AMERICAN BUSINESS ENGLISH

AMERICAN BUSINESS ENGLISH

Karen H. Bartell

Ann Arbor

THE UNIVERSITY OF MICHIGAN PRESS

ISBN 0-472-06608-0

Library of Congress Catalog Card No. 95-61196

Published in the United States of America by

The University of Michigan Press

Manufactured in the United States of America

2000   1999   1998   1997   5   4   3   2

To Peter Bartell, my graphic designer and husband,

and not necessarily in that order

PREFACE

Whether you're a novice writer, an inexperienced writer, or an accomplished writer, *AMERICAN BUSINESS ENGLISH* explains what you need to know. It takes you from start to finish, from the conception of ideas to the final editing process.

It takes you by the hand and walks you through all the basic strategies and techniques of writing. This book doesn't tell you, it SHOWS you how to create ideas and organize them. It concisely lists the rules for punctuation, spelling, and parts of speech.

It describes how to choose the right words, construct those words into sentences, and then build those sentences into paragraphs.

This book offers advice, examples, and exercises on every form of business writing, from meeting agendas and minutes to in-house memos, letters, and business correspondence. More importantly, it describes how to plan, structure, and write short reports, long reports, business proposals, and even manuals.

This all-inclusive book on business writing points out the precise style, tone, and tactics for use at every level of business communication. It offers you blueprints, formulas, and examples for each topic discussed.

However, this is MORE than a reference book. It's a tutorial, including exercises to practice your newly learned skills.

Finally this book explains how to refine your writing through correct editing and rewriting processes. It's the A to Z of writing. Because it's user-friendly, providing simple step-by-step instructions for every type of written communication, this is the ONLY book you'll ever need for all your business writing.

CONTENTS

1 WRITING STRATEGIES   **1**

Be Specific • Be Concrete • Be Clear • Be Objective • Be Specific

2 POINT OF VIEW   **6**

Audience • Goals

3 WRITING AND ORGANIZATION   **8**

Beginning, Middle, and Ending • Formal Formula for Writing • Correspondence of Formal Report Style • Informal Formula for Writing (Karen's Hamburger Theory)

4 TECH WRITING TECHNIQUES   **14**

White Space • Headers or Titles • Subtitles • Short Paragraphs • Short Sentences • Completeness • Perfection

5 CREATING AND GENERATING IDEAS   **19**

Generating Ideas

6 ARRANGING IDEAS EFFECTIVELY   **23**

OR LIMNING

7 PUNCTUATION POINTERS   **25**

OR HOW TO BECOME COMMA-TOSE

Commas • Periods • Semicolons • Colons • Dashes • Question Marks • Exclamation Marks • Quotation Marks • Apostrophes

8 WORDS AND HOW THEY WORK   **42**

Tone • Form

9 PARTS AND PARCELS OF SPEECH   **56**

Nouns • The Case for Pronouns • Adjectives • Lights, Cameras, Verbs! • Adverbs • Prepositions • Conjunctions • Interjections

10 SENTENCES   76
AND THEIR CRAFTSMANSHIP
Purpose • Composition • Classification • Sentence Errors •
Agreement • Collective Nouns

11 PARAGRAPHS AND PARANOIA   88
Topic Sentences • Supporting Sentences • Concluding
Sentences • Transitional Sentences • Paragraph Forms •
Emphasis • Objectivity • Subjectivity

12 MEETINGS, AGENDAS, AND MINUTES   106
Sample Agenda • Minutes Format

13 BUSINESS CORRESPONDENCE   113
OR LETTER WRITING
Letter Structure and Content • Letter Layout or Format • Letter
Tone and Style • Mechanics of Letters • Envelopes

14 CATEGORIES OF BUSINESS LETTERS   138
Letters of Query, Request • Letters of Complaint, Claim, and
Adjustment • Sales Letters or Direct Mailings

15 IN-HOUSE MEMOS   155
AND SHORT REPORTS
Layout: The Parts of a Memo or Short Report • Purposes of
Memos • Kinds of Memos

16 LONG REPORTS AND MANUALS   163
OR PLANNING GUIDELINES
Select Topic and Limit Scope • Brainstorm • List Sources of
Information • Note Random Pieces of Information • Organize
Information or Classy Classification • Limn or Outline Long
Reports/Manuals • Write Rough Draft • Edit Several Times •
Rewrite • Assemble Final Bibliography • Create Table of
Contents • Optional Parts of a Long Report or Manual

17 **REPORTS' TONE:**   **171**

LEVELS OF FORMALITY

Language • Contractions • Abbreviations • Personal Pronouns •
Passive Voice • Your Audience

18 **WRITING STYLES**   **175**

FOR LONG REPORTS OR MANUALS

Comparison/Contrast • Process • Analysis • Description •
Argument and Persuasion

19 **EDITING, REWRITING, AND POLISHING**   **193**

The Invisible Writing System of Editing

20 **GRAPHICS**   **207**

OR A PICTURE'S WORTH A THOUSAND WORDS

Types of Graphics • Graph Writing Techniques

ANSWER KEY   **220**

GLOSSARY   **226**

RECOMMENDED READING   **229**

WRITING STRATEGIES

1

The first thing you need to know about business writing is how to express yourself with the fewest words. **Be concise!** Write to be clearly understood, to express, not to impress. To best illustrate the idea, this book is written in that style.

BE SPECIFIC — SPECIFICITY

Say what you mean. Clearly. Don't be vague or confusing.

BE	DON'T BE
Concrete	Abstract
Clear	Confusing
Objective	Subjective
Specific	General

Remember—the purpose of writing is to communicate ideas.

- Think through exactly what you want to say. Organize your thoughts.
- Choose words that will best express your thoughts. Be clear.

BE CONCRETE — NOT ABSTRACT

Good writing is CONCRETE not ABSTRACT. Good writing uses facts, not vague descriptions.

Concrete:

> The _ABC Company_ purchased _12,000 shares of IBM_ on the _1st of September._

Abstract:

> _They_ bought _some stocks last month._

Concrete:

> The _sun shone brightly in the clear sky,_ while the _temperature rose to 33 degrees._

Abstract:

> The day was _nice_ and _hot._

Things are concrete. Ideas are abstract.

Objects are concrete. Qualities are abstract.

Concrete words tell exactly what you mean. They refer to objects which can be touched, smelled, heard, tasted, or seen. Names, facts, figures, and numbers are all concrete.

Things: _Tuesday, hair, 94, seven inches, 6.2%, 7:00 P.M., fog, March 4th, sweat, socks, smoke, chocolate, jazz._

Abstract words are not effective in expressing your message. They refer to ideas which cannot be touched, smelled, heard, tasted, or seen. Because abstract words only partly describe your meaning, they don't convince your reader of your message.

Ideas: _Good, nice, bad, lots, some, large, happy, terrible, wonderful, love, hate, handsome, beautiful._

EXERCISE FOR CONCRETE AND ABSTRACT WORDS

Separate the concrete words from the abstract.

bitter	shirts	rich
snow	chilly	sunshine
exciting	humid	modern
green	six	ugly

Concrete:_____   Abstract:_____

_____   _____

_____   _____

_____   _____

_____   _____

EXERCISE FOR GENERAL TO SPECIFIC ORDER

Arrange these phrases in the order of the most general to the most specific.
Number 1 is the most general; number 9 is the most specific.

____	tall people
____	a tall boy
____	tall boys
____	John Smith, who is 6' 3" tall
1	tallness
____	the tall boy
____	the boy who is 6' 3" tall
____	John, who is 6' 3" tall
____	a boy 6' 3" tall

BE CLEAR — NOT CONFUSING

Good writing is CLEAR not CONFUSING.

Choose words that are direct. Don't use big words when small words will do. It's better to write with one-syllable words correctly than to use six-syllable words incorrectly.

Use short, clear sentences. Don't use long sentences when short ones will be more easily understood by your audience. Complex and compound sentence structures may be good for the classroom, but simple sentence structures are better for the boardroom: Subject, Verb, Object.

BE OBJECTIVE — NOT SUBJECTIVE

Good writing is OBJECTIVE not SUBJECTIVE.

Objective means that all people have the same definition and understanding of a particular word.

33°C

Thirty-three degrees Celsius has the same meaning for all people. Hot, on the other hand, has a different interpretation for each person.

Someone described as weighing 145 kilograms is considered quite heavy; all people would have the same understanding of that person's weight. Someone described as fat could be imagined differently by each person.

145 kgs.

Subjective means that each person has a different definition or understanding of a word.

Simply put, objective *is*, but subjective is ***thought to be***. Be careful to use objective words in your writing.

BE SPECIFIC   —   NOT GENERAL

Good writing is SPECIFIC not GENERAL.

Use precisely the words you need, and you can write with fewer words. Describe your product or service exactly, and you'll avoid any misunderstandings. By being specific, you prove what you write because you present facts. Facts avoid confusion.

Don't write about a subject using general statements. **Be specific.** If you want to discuss stock investments, pick one particular stock and describe it in detail; don't write about Wall Street. If you want to discuss blue jeans, write about the designers and denim; don't write about the entire textile industry.

To best communicate your ideas, write in detail about one specific part or area; don't write about the whole.

Don't write about the whole pie; only describe one small slice.

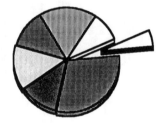

One specific example can communicate an idea more effectively than can general statements. Too broad a statement can lead to stereotypes.

GENERAL:

Stocks are risky investments.

SPECIFIC:

XYZ stocks rose six points during the first quarter, then fell 18 points within the following 24 hour period.

POINT OF VIEW

2

Before you write anything, think of two things:

Who am I writing to?   **AUDIENCE**

What do I want from them?   **GOALS**

AUDIENCE

First decide who your audience will be. Choose words that are appropriate for that audience. If your audience is composed of doctors, for instance, you can use words such as <u>medulla oblongata</u>. If your audience is composed of nonmedical people, you would do better to use the word <u>brain</u>.

If your audience is made up of computer buffs, use words such as <u>baud rate</u>, <u>stop bits</u>, and <u>parity</u>. If your audience is made up of noncomputer types, use words like <u>settings</u>. When writing for peers or coworkers, use the technical jargon or words of your profession; when not, use terms that can be understood by anyone.

Try to write from your readers' point of view. If you want to sell computers, slant your writing to describe why it would be beneficial *to them* to purchase your computer. Write so that the persons reading it can relate to it, can see it from their own perspectives.

GOALS

Keep your goal or your purpose for writing in mind. Although you will write from your readers' point of view, remember what it is you want from your audience.

Is your goal to have another company invest in yours? Describe how their company can benefit, how your company can help *them*.

Do you want to convince the Board of Directors that expansion is necessary? Then show them with examples, facts, and graphics how expansion will profit the company, will help *them*.

Remember Two Things:

1. Write from your readers' point of view.
2. Conclude your report with a request for what you want.
   (This is known as a CALL FOR ACTION.)

> Lee Iacocca wrote that he never ended a presentation without asking for something. He knew what he wanted. He asked for it.

Write from your audience's point of view.

Ask for What You Want

The true value of your writing is its effectiveness in reaching *YOUR* goals. Writing is your tool for getting what you want.

Prepared with this background, word choice, point of view, and goals for writing, you are now ready to write.

WRITING AND ORGANIZATION 3

Good writing requires good organization. Whether writing a memo, report, or manual, you need to organize your material and present it in a way that will make sense to your readers.

> The Greek philosopher, Aristotle, said all writing requires three things:
> - ☐ a beginning
> - ☐ a middle
> - ☐ an end

BEGINNING, MIDDLE, AND ENDING

These three things correspond today with an *introduction*, a *body* of material, and a *conclusion*. Writing is that simple.

Your writing needs a beginning, a middle, and an ending. Another way of making this point is to say:

- Tell your audience what you are going to tell them.
- Tell your audience.
- Tell your audience what you have told them.

In other words:

- **Introduce your material**
- **Present your material**
- **Summarize your material**

FORMAL FORMULA FOR WRITING
The Outline

Paragraph 1,
also known as the **INTRODUCTION**,
includes three things:
- Reader Interest
- Statement of Purpose
- Synopsis of Topics

Transition

Paragraph 2,
also known as the **BODY**,
includes two things:
- Topic Sentence
- Support Sentence

Transition

Paragraph 3,
also known as the **BODY**,
includes two things:
- Topic Sentence
- Support Sentence

Transition

Paragraph 4,
also known as the **BODY**,
includes two things:
- Topic Sentence
- Support Sentence

Transition

Paragraph 5,
also known as the **CONCLUSION**,
includes three things:
- Summary of Body/Topics
- Restatement of Purpose
- Call to Action

Introduction

The introductory paragraph is composed of three things:

- An opening sentence that grabs the readers' interest.
- A statement of purpose or the reason you are writing.
- A synopsis or sketch of the topics you will be discussing.

Body

The body of the writing may include a minimum of three paragraphs or as many paragraphs as are needed to explain your material. Each of these paragraphs is composed of four things:

- An opening topic sentence which includes the most important fact of that topic.
  - Only one topic per paragraph!
  - Several paragraphs may be used for each topic.
- Support sentences that further explain or prove the topic.
- Concluding sentence which summarizes that topic.
- Transitions that occur at the end of each paragraph.

  (Transitions help your readers go from one idea to the next.)

For more information regarding paragraph construction, see the **PARAGRAPHS AND PARANOIA** section. **CHAPTER 11**

Conclusion

The concluding paragraph is composed of three things:

- A summary of the body or the topics.
- A restatement of purpose.
- A call to action from your readers.

THIS IS WHERE YOU STATE WHAT YOU WANT.

CORRESPONDENCE OF FORMAL REPORT STYLE

Paragraph   THREE PARTS OF A REPORT:

1 Introduction: **INTRODUCTION**

- Statement of Purpose
- Three (or more) topics
  (in fragmentary form)

2 First Topic: **BODY**

- Topic Sentence
- Support for Topic Sentence
- Concluding Sentence
  (Transition)

3 Second Topic:

- Topic Sentence
- Support for Topic Sentence
- Concluding Sentence
  (Transition)

4 Third Topic:

- Topic Sentence
- Support for Topic Sentence
- Concluding Sentence
  (Transition)

5 Conclusion: **CONCLUSION**

- Summary of Topics
- Restatement of Purpose
- Call to Action

Following is an example to illustrate this Formal Formula:

Paragraph 1 *Because people have been curious for centuries, I want to explain why the heavens contain blue skies. The sky is blue for three reasons: sunshine, clear skies, and no rain.*

Paragraph 2 *Sunshine causes blue skies. The sun's rays dry the moisture from the air. This eliminates clouds.*

Paragraph 3 *Clear skies allow the blue color of the sky to shine through. Clear skies are cloudless skies. Skies without clouds cannot rain.*

Paragraph 4 *No rain keeps the sky from looking gray; the color blue shows clearly. No rain means fair weather.*

Paragraph 5 *Because of these three reasons, sunshine, clear skies, and no rain, the sky is blue. People can now understand how and why the sky is blue. Look up at the sky and enjoy its blue beauty.*

Notice in the **introductory** paragraph how reader interest was established, how the statement of purpose was made, and how the three synopsized topics were introduced.

Notice how those three topics were lengthened into topic sentences, or opening sentences, in the following three paragraphs. After each topic sentence came support sentences. Each of the paragraphs of the **body** ended with a transition or a sentence that took the reader from that paragraph's idea to the next.

Notice how the final paragraph, or the **conclusion**, restated the topics and restated the purpose for writing the paper. Most important of all, notice how it concluded with a ***call for action.***

This is the Formal Formula. Now compare it with my Informal Formula.

INFORMAL FORMULA FOR WRITING

Karen's Hamburger Theory—You have never seen this before! I am drawing an analogy, or making a comparison, between writing a paper and fixing a hamburger.

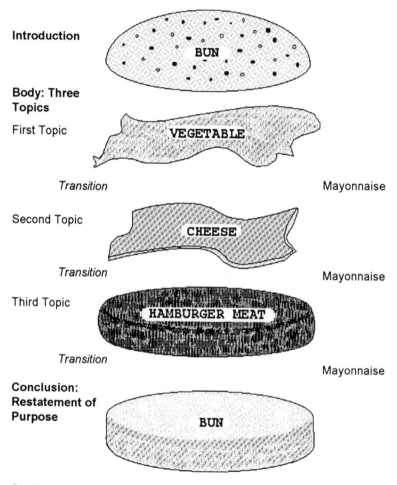

Introduction

BUN

Body: Three Topics

First Topic

VEGETABLE

Transition   Mayonnaise

Second Topic

CHEESE

Transition   Mayonnaise

Third Topic

HAMBURGER MEAT

Transition

                                                         Mayonnaise

Conclusion: Restatement of Purpose

BUN

See how the hamburger is surrounded by a bun, both underneath and on top? The top bun is the introduction; the bottom bun is the conclusion. Between the buns is the body: the vegetable, cheese, and meat. These compare with the three topics in the body of a paper. The mayonnaise relates to the transitions between paragraphs because both cause the parts to *slide smoothly.*

TECH WRITING TECHNIQUES 4

Good business writing requires good technical writing.
Tech writing techniques include seven things:

- White Space
- Headers or Titles
- Subtitles
- Short Paragraphs
- Short Sentences
- Completeness within itself
- Perfection

WHITE SPACE

White space simply means the white paper which shows through the typed words. Don't let your writing have a cluttered look about it. Keep margins wide, and keep the text short. Use as few words as possible. A page full of black characters is frightening to readers. White space makes the writing **appear** more user-friendly.

Style

Leave wide margins

When report is bound at the *left*:

Top margin	1"		Right margin	1"
Left margin	1.5"		Bottom margin	1"

When report is bound at the *top*:

Top margin	2"	(First page)	Right margin	1"
Top margin	1"	(Other pages)	Bottom margin	1"
Left margin	1"			

Have wide indentations for indented paragraphs—Five spaces

Long, quoted passages:

- Indent five spaces from left
- Indent five spaces from right
- Single space between lines
- Omit quotation marks

Also:

- Double space between lines
- Double space between paragraphs
- First page of report is not numbered
- All remaining pages are numbered

Paging

- Bound at left—Four lines from top at right margin
- Bound at top—Seven lines from bottom, centered

TITLE PAGE

Center material:

- Name of report
- Author of report
- Business or institution
- Date of presentation
- Name of person/department presented to

Use asterisks (∗) or bullets (■) to designate items in a list

List key words instead of writing complete sentences

HEADERS OR TITLES

A header is another word for a title. Use headers often. They make it easier for readers to grasp your ideas at a glance. Your busy audience will not read your report or proposal if it LOOKS too difficult to understand. Titles, however, identify the basic ideas, the most important ideas. Because they're easy to comprehend, titles invite your audience to read on. Perception is everything. The easier it looks, the more your audience will read.

SUBTITLES

Subtitles are a second means for your audience to grasp your ideas without actually reading *every* word in your report. A subtitle appears on the line above almost every paragraph. It summarizes the topic of the paragraph(s). A speed reader will read only titles, subtitles, lists, and topic sentences. Compress your main ideas into key phrases, then use them as subtitles. Another way of describing this process is to *name* the topic of the paragraph(s), then use it as the subtitle.

SHORT PARAGRAPHS

Keep your paragraphs short. Use only one idea per paragraph. If the idea is complex, write another or even several more paragraphs describing only one aspect of the idea in each paragraph. Make it easy for the reader to follow your thoughts.

If using block-style writing, double space or leave a blank line between each paragraph instead of indenting. If indenting, begin each paragraph five spaces from the left margin.

SHORT SENTENCES

Keep your sentences short and to the point. To do this, use simple sentence structure and the active voice. The easier it is for your readers to understand your writing, the more they will read.

Simple Sentences

A simple sentence has one main clause and no subordinate clauses. The structure of a simple sentence is <u>Subject</u>, <u>Verb</u>, <u>Object</u>.

S V O

He went home.

They sold 20,000 shares.

She invested the money.

Use simple sentences. Save the compound and complex sentences for your fictional writing, not your business writing. You want your readers to understand your ideas, not be impressed by your writing.

For more information on sentence structure, refer to the **SENTENCES AND THEIR CRAFTSMANSHIP** section. **CHAPTER 10**

Active Voice

Use the active voice, not the passive. Your words will have greater impact with the direct style of the active voice. For this, also use the Subject-Verb-Object structure.

Active	*She invested the money.*	
	The money was invested by her.	**Passive**
	The money was invested.	**Passive**
Active	*We appreciate your cooperation.*	
	Your cooperation is appreciated by us.	**Passive**
	Your cooperation is appreciated. ·	**Passive**

Use the active voice.

The *active voice* is informative and interesting. A verb has an active voice when it describes an action done BY its subject.

The *passive voice* is vague and boring. A verb has a passive voice when it describes an action done TO its subject.

You want your audience to read through your material quickly. The *passive voice* slows down the reading speed. Remember, the easier, the better. The faster your audience can grasp your ideas, the more they'll read. Write for the reader.

For more information on verbs, refer to the **LIGHTS, CAMERAS, VERBS!** segment of the **PARTS AND PARCELS OF SPEECH** section. CHAPTER 9

COMPLETENESS

Include *all* the information in the report.

- Don't assume that your readers have any prior knowledge of the facts contained within your writing; **they don't.**

- Don't expect your readers to seek out additional information from other reports or memos; **they won't.**

PERFECTION

That's right. Aim for perfection. Edit your writing to make sure it's free of grammatical errors or misspelled words. Proofread your material to be sure it contains no typos or typing mistakes.

Polish your writing until it "disappears." The best writing is invisible. In other words, the best writing has no errors to interrupt the flow of ideas from the author to the reader.

For more information about editing and proofreading, see the **EDITING, REWRITING, AND POLISHING** section. **CHAPTER 19**

EXERCISE FOR ACTIVE/PASSIVE VOICES

The following sentences are in the passive voice. Change the sentences to the more forceful, active voice.

1. The report was written by Sam because Jules had made the speech.

_____

2. The car was waxed and polished by the driver.

_____

3. Joan was known by all her colleagues, and she was respected by everyone.

_____

4. The new tuxedo was worn by him to the business function.

_____

5. The case against the embezzler was dropped by the FBI for lack of evidence.

_____

CREATING AND GENERATING IDEAS 5

Rules for syntax and grammar, organizational tips, and spelling hints only help **after** you know what you are going to write. This section SHOWS YOU HOW to get ideas for writing and how to arrange these ideas in the most effective order. Instead of telling you, this chapter SHOWS you two things:

■ How to generate ideas

■ How to arrange those ideas effectively

GENERATING IDEAS

Free-writing

The Chinese say that a journey of a thousand miles begins with the first step. Getting started is the most difficult part. Often the ideas are trapped inside your mind, and you can't access them.

The quickest way of accessing that material is to free-write. Sit in a quiet room with only a pen (not a pencil or eraser), paper, and a watch. Allow yourself only ten minutes, no more. Begin writing.

That's it. Just write about any subject without paying attention to grammatical form, organization, or spelling. (That's why you use a pen and ink—not a pencil or eraser.) Don't worry about errors. Don't stop to think. Don't worry about what to write. Just write. For ten minutes.

It may take a moment before the words begin flowing rapidly, but they will. You'll be amazed at what brilliant material comes out of your pen. Don't be judgmental. Don't be critical. Just write.

You can edit or correct the punctuation and grammatical errors later. For now, just write. At the end of ten minutes, you will have the basis for your report. Often the hardest thing is just getting started. This method eliminates the hard part. Just do it. Just begin.

EXERCISE FOR FREE-WRITING

You need these items:

⇒ Pen

⇒ Paper

⇒ Watch (ten minutes)

Directions:

■ Write

■ Do not criticize

■ Do not stop to think

■ After ten minutes, put down your pen   (Edit only then)

Spread-Sheet Writing or Clustering

Sometimes you have a basic idea of what you want to write, but you can't think of any supporting ideas or subtopics. The best way to deal with that is to find a large piece of paper and write down your general topic. Draw a circle around it.

Next write down related ideas radiating outward from the central idea, like spokes from a wheel. Draw circles around them. Then think of other topics relating to those, and place them in a circular pattern, radiating out from the first round of ideas.

As an example, let's look at art:

Clustering or Spread-Sheet Writing

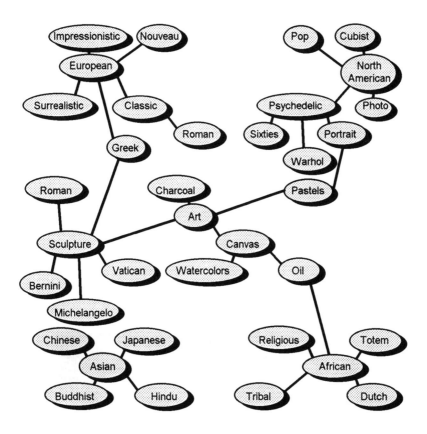

The items become more SPECIFIC as the items in the circles move farther away from the central idea.

Clustering helps in two ways:

- To **GENERATE** ideas.
- To **LIMIT** the topic.

Often this works best when combined with BRAINSTORMING, which means working together with others to come up with ideas. As they say, two heads are better than one; three are better than two; and four heads are better than three. Combine your knowledge with others', and the results will improve exponentially.

EXERCISE FOR SPREAD-SHEET WRITING OR CLUSTERING

You need these items:

⇒ Pen

⇒ Large sheet of paper (the bigger, the better)

Directions:

■ Brainstorm for ideas—(Think by yourself or with others)

■ Write idea names *only*—(The actual writing comes later)

Just as Spread-Sheet writing *increases* ideas, it can also be used to *limit* ideas. Sometimes a topic seems too broad. In that case, your writing will improve by limiting the scope of that report. Use this same method to narrow and focus a subject.

Remember, it's more effective to write thoroughly about one small slice of a pie than to write generally about the whole pie. Choose the "slice," or the limited topic, which is best suited for your purpose by using this Spread-Sheet method.

Arranging Ideas Effectively

or Limning

6

After you have your most important ideas and their related, supporting ideas, you need a way to organize them. The best method for arranging ideas is to limn them. Artists do this all the time.

They sketch their ideas, using as few strokes of the brush as possible. Take your cue from artists. Sketch your ideas using as few strokes of the pen as possible. Outline your thoughts.

I. First Major Idea
   1. First Supporting Division
   2. Second Supporting Division
II. Second Major Idea
   1. First Supporting Division
   2. Second Supporting Division
III. Third Major Idea
   1. First Supporting Division
      a. First Supplementary Division
      b. Second Supplementary Division
   2. Second Supporting Division
      a. First Supplementary Division
      b. Second Supplementary Division
         1. First Detailed Division
         2. Second Detailed Division
            (a). First Supporting Detailed Division
            (b). Second Supporting Detailed Division
               i. First Sub-detail
               ii. Second Sub-detail

It is much easier to move ideas around before they are fleshed out with words. Use the limning method of outlining before you begin the actual process of writing.

Seeing all the ideas on one page also helps to organize their flow. Arrange the ideas so that the parts follow a logical sequence in becoming the whole. Arrange them so the reader can easily follow your ideas in their progression.

EXERCISE FOR LIMNING

Try limning or outlining a subject. Use "Art," for example, as your main topic. Either think of your own Supporting Divisions and Detailed Divisions, or refer to Chapter 5, "Creating and Generating Ideas," for ideas.

_____

_____

_____

_____

_____

_____

_____

_____

_____

_____

_____

_____

_____

_____

PUNCTUATION POINTERS

OR HOW TO BECOME COMMA-TOSE

Punctuation is often considered so boring that it can put a person to sleep, almost making that person comatose. Commas can make a person comma-tose.

Still, no book on writing would be complete without a reference section for punctuation. Nine punctuation marks will be explained and demonstrated in this section:

1. Commas
2. Periods
3. Semicolons
4. Colons
5. Dashes
6. Question Marks
7. Exclamation Marks
8. Quotation Marks
9. Apostrophes

COMMAS

Commas should be used sparingly. When in doubt, leave them out. Commas are used in writing the way pauses are used in speaking. They tell the reader to stop momentarily, to pause.

Actually, commas are simple to use. They have only four uses:

- To join two sentences with a coordinator
- To set off a subordinate clause or phrase from the independent clause
- To separate items in a series or list
- To mark letter salutations and closings (hellos and goodbyes)

When joining two sentences, a comma precedes the coordinator. Use a comma BEFORE a coordinator.

Coordinators, also known as coordinating conjunctions, are the words and, but, or, nor, for, yet.

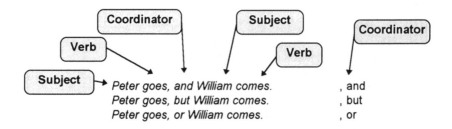

Peter goes, and William comes.	, and
Peter goes, but William comes.	, but
Peter goes, or William comes.	, or

Do not use a comma for compound verbs or subjects.

| *Peter goes and comes.* | compound verbs |
| *Peter and William go.* | compound subjects |

When setting off a subordinate clause or phrase from the independent clause, a comma follows the subordinate clause or phrase. Use a comma AFTER the subordinate clause or phrase.

A partial list of subordinators, also known as subordinating conjunctions, follows:

after	although	as	as much as
because	before	how	if
inasmuch as	in order that	provided	since
so that	that	than	though
till	unless	until	when
whenever	where	wherever	while

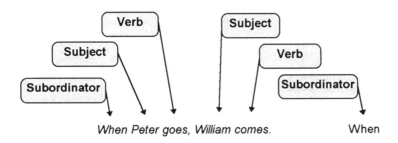

When Peter goes, William comes.   When

If the subordinator appears in the middle of the sentence, do not use a comma.

Peter goes when William comes.

Commas also follow introductory phrases (intro phrases).

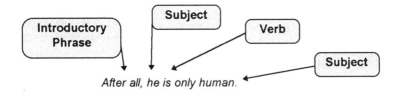

After all, he is only human.

In this same line of thought, a comma can also be used after a transitional expression.

Space

Several partial lists of transitional expressions, also known as qualifiers, follow:

(To restrict or limit space.)

adjacent to	beyond	further
here	in the middle	nearby
next to	opposite to	there
to the left/right	where	wherever

Summary

(To summarize ideas or restate topic ideas.)

as a result	as can be seen	as shown above
consequently	for this reason	for these reasons
generally speaking	hence	in any case
in any event	in brief	in conclusion
in either case	in fact	in short
on the whole	therefore	thus

Support

(To give illustrations or examples.)

as	for example	for instance
in fact	in general	such as

Time

(To define, limit, or restrict time.)

after	at the present time	at the same time
at this point	before	during
eventually	finally	first/second/etc.
further	hence	henceforth
in due time	in time	later
meanwhile	once	since
sooner or later	then	to begin with
until	until now	whenever

Commas can be used to separate items in a series or a list.

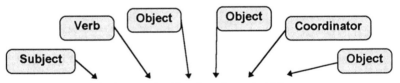

John has cooked beef, pork, and chicken.
He parks cars in the driveway, on the road, or at the curb.
Looking successful, feeling successful, and being successful
demand hard work.

If a coordinator appears between each of the items, do not use a comma.

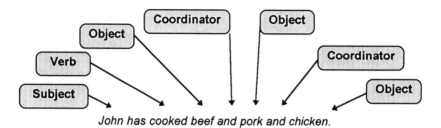

John has cooked beef and pork and chicken.

A comma is used to punctuate the salutation of an informal letter and the closing of any letter. Use a comma AFTER these:

> *Dear John,*
> *Very truly yours,*

A colon is used after the salutation of a business letter:

> *Dear Mr. Jones:*

EXERCISE FOR COMMAS

Place commas where needed in the following sentences:

1. The midwestern states involved in our project are Wisconsin Michigan Illinois and Indiana.

2. The truck approached a wide smooth span of highway.

3. The company invested wisely and the dividends paid well.

4. Ms. Jones ordered coffee and eggs and toast for breakfast.

5. The insurance policy covered disability maternity leave and durable equipment in the employees' benefits.

PERIODS

Periods are easy to use because they are applied in only two ways:

    1.   To end a statement

    2.   To end an abbreviation

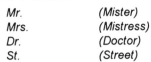

Use a period AT THE END of a sentence or complete thought.

> *John stayed home today.*
> *Letter writing is easy.*

Use a period AT THE END of an abbreviation.

Mr.	*(Mister)*
Mrs.	*(Mistress)*
Dr.	*(Doctor)*
St.	*(Street)*

SEMICOLONS

Using semicolons is an easy way to increase your collection of sentence patterns. Once you feel familiar with this punctuation, you'll enjoy the variety of expression it allows you.

Semicolons are used in four ways:

    1. Between main clauses that are NOT joined by

        and, but, or, nor, for, yet

    2. Between main clauses that ARE joined by

accordingly	also	besides
consequently	for example	for instance
furthermore	hence	however
instead	moreover	nevertheless
otherwise	still	that is
thus		

    3. Between main clauses if commas are used in the clauses

    4. Between items in a series if the items contain commas

Semicolons are used between main clauses that are NOT joined by the words <u>and</u>, <u>but</u>, <u>or</u>, <u>nor</u>, <u>for</u>, <u>yet</u>.

> S V   O ; S V   O
> *I like candy; I love chocolate.*

A semicolon may be used to connect two sentences that would otherwise be punctuated with a period. Use a semicolon instead of a period (and a capital letter) when the sentences are closely related.

> *This house is red. That house is green.*
> *This house is red; that house is green.*

Remember, sentences may be related in three ways:

1. *I like candy. I love chocolate.*   (a period)
2. *I like candy; I love chocolate.*   (a semicolon)
3. *I like candy, and I love chocolate.*   (a comma + <u>and</u>)

Use a semicolon if the two ideas are closely related.

Use a semicolon between main clauses that ARE joined by connectives.

> *I like candy; for instance, I love chocolate.*
> *This house is red; however, that house is green.*
> *I like candy; therefore I eat it.*

When placed at the beginning of a clause, some connectives are not followed by a comma. If these words interrupt a clause, they must be followed by a comma.

These words are ALWAYS followed by a comma:

> *for example*   *for instance*   *however*   *that is*

Use a semicolon if commas are used in the clauses.

> *Scarlett, a character in the book <u>Gone With the Wind</u>, was spirited, strong-willed, and compulsive; and her husbands, understandably, were cooperative, complacent people.*

Use a semicolon in a series if the items contain commas.

> *The following characters were in the book <u>Gone With the Wind</u>: Scarlett, the main character; Ashley, the love of her life; Charles, her first husband; Frank, her second husband; and, finally, Rhett, her third husband.*

EXERCISE FOR SEMICOLONS

Add semicolons to these sentences or, when necessary, replace commas or words with semicolons to correct the following sentences:

1. In the morning, I like melon, I prefer apples.

_____

2. He got up early, and he dressed before breakfast.

_____

3. They had lunch then they went back to work.

_____

4. The bus was crowded; and the taxis wouldn't stop.

_____

5. Sam ordered a hamburger, fries, and a coke, Jane ordered a salad, a croissant, and tea, Tim only wanted coffee.

_____

COLONS

Colons are used to announce things, much the way trumpets announce the arrival of important people or events. Colons are meant to draw attention to what follows.

There are five main uses for colons:

1.   To introduce lists

2.   To announce long or formal statements

3.   To divide two statements of the same idea

4.   To use between numbers, volumes, pages, chapters, verses

5.   To use after a formal salutation (Dear Ms. Jones:)

Lists

A colon may be used to introduce lists. Often the words <u>as follows</u> or <u>the following</u> will appear before the colon.

>*My five favorite characters of <u>Gone With the Wind</u> are as follows: Scarlett, Ashley, Charles, Frank, and Rhett.*

Announcing

A colon may be used to announce long or formal statements. When quoting people, this is often an effective substitution for quotation marks.

>*Lee Iacocca made the following statement: The primary skill of a manager consists of knowing how to make assignments and picking the right people to carry out those assignments.*

Division

A colon may be used to divide two statements of the same idea when the second clause restates or further explains the first.

>*The computers have modems: these communications devices allow computers to transmit information over telephone lines.*

Book titles are often punctuated this way, where one formal aspect of an idea is followed by an informal aspect.

>*<u>Horticulture and Money:</u>*
>*<u>Money Doesn't Grow on Trees</u>*

Between Numbers...

A colon may be used between numbers, volumes, pages, chapters, and verses.

>*4:30 P.M.*
>*Harper's 202:114–21*
>*Genesis 1:3*

Salutation

A colon may be used after a formal salutation in a business letter.

>*Dear Ms. Jones:*
>*Gentlemen:*

A colon is used in a formal letter, but a comma is used in an informal letter. (Dear John,)

DASHES

A dash is often used <u>informally</u> the same way a colon is used formally. Avoid using dashes in business writing: they appear unprofessional or amateurish. Remember that perception is everything in the business world of writing. Limit your use of dashes to informal personal notes or letters.

Use dashes in two circumstances:

1. To indicate a pause in thought
2. To indicate a transitional expression

Pause

A dash may be used to indicate a pause in thought. This will help allow the reader to follow your line of thinking.

I could—and if all goes well, will—buy that convertible.

Transition

A dash may be used in place of a transitional expression. In informal circumstances, a dash may be used instead of a phrase such as <u>therefore</u>, <u>that is</u>, <u>i.e.</u>, <u>in other words</u>.

I want to buy that car—I will buy that car if I close the deal.

EXERCISE FOR COLONS AND DASHES

Add the necessary colons, dashes, and commas to the following sentences:

1. Our bowling team there are eight of us went to the bowling alley at 730 and stayed until 1000.
2. John bought the book *How to Cook A Manual for Bachelors* just the kind of book he needs.
3. The XYZ Company ordered the following chairs, desks, computers.
4. Tom needed everything a refrigerator, a stove, a washing machine.
5. Dear Mrs. Jones   Dear Susan

QUESTION MARKS

Simply put, question marks are placed at the end of questions. More specifically, there are three uses for question marks:

1. In <u>direct</u> questions
2. In polite requests in question form
3. Inside and outside quotation marks

Direct Questions

A question mark is used at the end of direct (vs. indirect) questions.

> *When is the report due?*
>
> (Direct. A question mark is necessary.)
>
> *He wants to know when the report is due.*
>
> (Indirect. No question mark is necessary.)

Polite Requests

A question mark is used in polite requests that are phrased in question form. Occasionally in business letters an order is phrased like a question. In this situation a period is acceptable, but a question mark is more polite. Perception is everything.

> *Can you deliver the order a week from tomorrow.*
>
> *Can you deliver the order a week from tomorrow?*

Quotation Marks

A question mark is used <u>inside</u> quotation marks when the quotation is a question. It is used <u>outside</u> quotation marks when the sentence surrounding the quotation asks a question.

> *She asked, "When is the report due?"*
>
> (Inside. The quotation is a question.)
>
> *Did she say, "The report is due"?*
>
> (Outside. The quotation itself is not a question, but the sentence surrounding it is.)

EXCLAMATION MARKS

An exclamation mark follows words that express excitement or strong emotions such as anger, relief, joy, fear, or surprise.

You look great!
I closed the deal!
That's wonderful!
Congratulations!

An exclamation mark is used <u>inside</u> quotation marks when the quotation is an exclamation. It is used <u>outside</u> quotation marks when the sentence surrounding the quotation is an exclamation.

She said, "The deal is closed!"
(Inside. The quotation is an exclamation.)

It's wonderful that she said, "The deal is closed"!
(Outside. The quotation itself is not an exclamation, but the sentence surrounding it is.)

QUOTATION MARKS

Quotation marks are used primarily to enclose direct quotes or the exact words of people. Use this punctuation in two ways:

1. To enclose direct quotations
2. To enclose titles of <u>parts</u> of books or magazines

Quotations

Quotation marks are used to enclose <u>direct</u> quotations or the exact words of people. Quotation marks are not used to enclose <u>indirect</u> quotations or words that are not the exact words of people.

She said, "Finish the report by noon."
(Direct. Use quotation marks. These are her exact words.)

She said that we should finish the report by noon.
(Indirect. Do not use quotation marks. These are similar words but not her exact words.)

Several punctuation rules apply to using quotation marks:

1. Begin each direct quotation with a capitalized letter.

    He said, "The report is fine."

2. If a quoted sentence is interrupted by the phrase <u>he said</u>, <u>she asked</u>, <u>they replied</u>, begin the second part with a small letter.

    "If the report is fine," he said, "go home early."

3. If the second part of the quoted sentence <u>is</u> a new sentence, begin with a capitalized letter.

    *"The report is fine," he said. "**Go** home early."*

4. Set off a quotation from the rest of the sentence with commas.

    He said, "The report is fine."
    "The report is fine," he said.
    "The report," he said, "is fine."

5. Place commas and periods inside quotation marks.

    "The report," he said, "is fine."

6. Place semicolons and colons outside quotation marks.

    "The report," he said, "is fine"; then he asked me to be vice president.

    He said to learn these "technical terms": pixel, pel, and protocol.

7. Place question marks and exclamation marks inside the quotation marks <u>only if</u> they are part of the quotation.

    "Is the report ready?" she asked.
    Were you happy when he said, "The report's ready"?

    "The report's ready!" he said.
    You were happy when he said, "The report's ready"!

Books and Magazines

Use quotation marks around parts of books and magazines. Enclose chapter titles and short story titles of books. Enclose article names of magazines or journals.

> *Make sure you read Chapter 21, "Program Manager," from our company manual, Computer Operations.*

> *This information is available in "The Tigers are Feeding on American Fare" in BusinessWeek.*

Underline or *italicize* titles of books and magazines. Use quotation marks around chapter titles or names of articles within magazines.

EXERCISE FOR QUESTION, EXCLAMATION, AND QUOTATION MARKS

Insert the proper question marks, exclamation marks, or quotation marks in the following sentences. Note that commas, periods, and capitalized letters will also be required at times.

1. She asked are you ready

2. Were you ready when she asked are you ready

3. Get going if you don't want to be late

4. Hurry up he said

5. I was nervous when he shouted no

APOSTROPHES

Apostrophes are used in two ways:

1. To show possession or ownership
2. To show a contraction or omission

Possession or Ownership

An apostrophe and an s̲ show possession or ownership.

SINGULAR NOUN

Add an apostrophe and an s̲

the boy's sweater   the dog's bark

PLURAL NOUN THAT ENDS IN S̲

Add an apostrophe only

the boys' sweaters   the dogs' food

IRREGULAR PLURAL NOUN THAT HAS NO FINAL S̲

Add an apostrophe and an s̲

women's shoes   firemen's hats

DISTANCE, MEASUREMENT, TIME, OR VALUE EXPRESSIONS

Add an apostrophe after plural expressions
Add an apostrophe and an s̲ after singular expressions

nine miles' distance   three months' notice
today's opportunity   a week's salary

ABBREVIATIONS

Place apostrophe and an s̲ after the period

Ph.D.'s dissertation   Columbia Co.'s books

COMPOUND WORDS

Add an apostrophe and an s̲ at the end

mother-in-law's home   mothers-in-law's homes

PLURAL LETTERS, NUMBERS, AND SYMBOLS

Add an apostrophe and an s̲

> *Don't forget to dot the i̲'s.*
> *There are three 7's in his phone number.*

JOINT OWNERSHIP

Use an apostrophe and an s̲ after the last of two or more nouns

> *Peter and John's car*   *Punch and Judy's antics*

INDIVIDUAL OWNERSHIP

Use an apostrophe and an s̲ after each noun

> *Peter's and John's cars*   *Punch's and Judy's antics*

INDEFINITE PRONOUNS

Add an apostrophe and an s̲

> *everyone's goal*   *everybody's idea*

Personal pronouns (his, hers, its, theirs, ours, yours, whose) do not need an apostrophe to show possession.

Contraction or Omission

Apostrophes are used in contractions of words.

> *haven't (have not)*
> *didn't (did not)*
> *he's (he is̲) or (he has̲)*

Apostrophes are used to show an omission.

> *'93 (1993)*

EXERCISE FOR APOSTROPHES

Place an apostrophe where it's needed:

1. Its Peters car.

2. Theyre part of Johns group.

3. Its time to celebrate 97.

4. Isnt that Janes house?

5. Didnt they say it was hers?

WORDS AND HOW THEY WORK

Many times you will know what you want to say, but you might have trouble expressing yourself. Either you are not sure what TONE to take or what FORM of the word to use. This chapter tackles these problems in two sections:

1. **TONE**—word choice for specific audiences

2. **FORM**—prefixes, suffixes, spelling

TONE

Tone is the way that something is expressed. Word choice largely determines tone. However, choosing the correct word for each audience is a skill, because another set will be more appropriate for a general audience.

Add a page footer.
> (Tone good for computer whizzes.)
> (Tone confusing for general public.)

Include the page number at the bottom of each page.
> (Tone more explanatory for a general audience.)
> (Tone too wordy for those familiar with jargon.)

Get that dog out of here!
> (Tone rude and imperative.)

Would you mind please taking the dog away?
> (Tone polite and questioning.)

The Tone Section includes three parts:

1. Abbreviations and Acronyms
2. Business-ese or Business Jargon
3. Wordiness

Abbreviations and Acronyms

Very few abbreviations are acceptable in business writing. When in doubt, spell it out. One notable exception is titles. When addressing people in business letters, it is perfectly acceptable to use abbreviations of their titles:

Used BEFORE the name:

Mr.	(Mister)	Mr. Teri James
Messrs.	(Plural of Mr.)	Messrs. James and Burr
Mrs.	(Married woman)	Mrs. Teri James
Mmes.	(Plural of Mrs.)	Mmes. James and Burr
Ms.	(Married OR unmarried woman)	Ms. Teri James
Dr.	(Doctor)	Dr. Teri James
Rev.	(Reverend)	Rev. Teri James
Hon.	(Honorable)	Hon. Teri James

Used AFTER the name:

M.D.	(Medical doctor)	Teri James, M.D.
Ph.D.	(Doctor of Philosophy)	Teri James, Ph.D.
M.A.	(Master of Arts)	Teri James, M.A.
Sr.	(Senior—the older OR the father)	Teri James, Sr.
Jr.	(Junior—the younger OR the son)	Teri James, Jr.
Esq.	(Attorney)	Teri James, Esq.
I	(The first)	Teri James I
II	(The second)	Teri James II

Other conventionally accepted abbreviations regard time:

A.M.	(Before noon—ante meridiem)	*9 A.M.*
P.M.	(Afternoon—post meridiem)	*3 P.M.*
A.D.	(In the year of our Lord—Anno Domini)	*A.D. 1023*
B.C.	(Before Christ)	*967 B.C.*

Avoid directional abbreviations in business writing:

street	*(St.)*
lane	*(Ln.)*
square	*(Sq.)*
avenue	*(Ave. or Av.)*
boulevard	*(Blvd.)*
north *(N.)*, south *(S.)*, east *(E.)*, west *(W.)*	

Acronyms are initials of words which form a new word, i.e.,

NEWS—North East West South
NATO—North Atlantic Treaty Organization

Acronyms are space-savers in business writing, but there is a particular way to use them:

- Spell out the entire phrase the first time it is used
- Indicate the initials in parentheses
- Use the acronym throughout the remainder of that writing

The North Atlantic Treaty Organization (NATO) will convene Monday. All NATO delegations will be present.

Exceptions to spelling out the entire name the first time are well-known business firms or agencies such as the following:

- **AT&T (American Telephone & Telegraph Company)**
- **FBI (Federal Bureau of Investigation)**
- **YMCA (Young Men's Christian Association)**

Business-ese or Business Jargon

Thinking it increases the importance of their writing, many business people use needlessly large words. However, instead of appearing more impressive, the writing seems pretentious. This "language" of the business world is called *Business-ese* or *jargon*.

For clear writing, AVOID jargon:

Jargon	Translation
advise	tell
aggregate	entire
ameliorate	improve
apportion	divide
classify	divide
collocate	collect
commence	begin
convene	meet
converse	talk
determine	decide
document	form
endeavor	try
exhibit	show
factor	point
forward	send
implement	begin
inaugurate	begin
indicate	show
initiate	begin
maximum	most
methodology	method
optimum	best
participate	join
peruse	read
presently	now
prioritize	choose priority
procedure	plan
subsequent	following
tender	give
terminate	stop
traverse	travel
utilize	use
viable	usable

Instead of using jargon, say what you mean and mean what you say.

Subject-specific jargon is all right with peers or business colleagues who are extremely familiar with that particular vocabulary. However, generally speaking, the larger the words, the more likely you are to confuse your audience. Keep it short.

EXERCISE FOR JARGON

Directions:

1. List fifteen words, terms, or phrases you use only in business.

2. Define these terms so a general audience could understand.

3. Justify the use of these terms for your peers.

4. Do they help or interfere with an exchange of knowledge?

Wordiness

Always get to the point!

Instead of using long prepositional phrases, omit extra words. Where one word clarifies an idea, five words complicate it,
   SO
use as few words as possible:

Use these:	Instead of these:
about	with reference to
about	as to
because	for the reason that
believe	are of the opinion
(a) check for	(a) check in the amount of
do	succeed in doing
during	during the course of
for (or to)	for the purpose of
go	go during the (winter) of
if (I can)	if I find it possible
information	information in the records
instead	in lieu of
like	along the lines of
make	succeed in making
need	would appreciate the benefit of
when	when in the course of

DO NOT be wordy or repetitious.

Avoid these:	**Use these:**
descending down	descending
far away in the distance	far away
great, huge	great OR huge
not audible to the ears	not audible
repeating again	repeating
returning back	returning
rising up	rising
this year's current	this year's OR the current
time-consuming delay	delay
visible to the eye	visible

**Be BRIEF, not wordy!
Be natural, not artificial!**

Sometimes novice writers use words in ways that sound artificial or stilted. Instead of stating their facts directly, they try to give their words added importance. They TRY too hard. As a result, the writing sounds affected or insincere.

Occasionally writers use stilted language to impress their readers because they think it sounds complex and accomplished. Instead the writing sounds pretentious or self-important.

Concentrate more on WHAT you write than HOW you write it. The idea is to inform your readers, not impress them.

EXPRESS: NOT IMPRESS

INFORM YOUR READERS: DON'T TRY TO IMPRESS THEM

Notice the difference:

> *The edifice was deluged with water.*

OR

> *The house was flooded.*

Which sentence makes the point more clearly?

For more information on tone, see the **REPORTS' TONE: LEVELS OF FORMALITY** section. **CHAPTER 17**

EXERCISE FOR WORDINESS

Rewrite the following paragraph, using as few words as possible. Omit all unnecessary words:

> In order to better facilitate your needs, it would perhaps be in the best interest of you and your firm to make use of an electrical apparatus such as the telephone instead of making use of the more involved and time consumptive method of putting pen to paper, as it were, and printing or typing your thoughts, questions, and suggestions.

_____

_____

_____

_____

_____

FORM

The Form Section includes three parts:

- Prefixes
- Suffixes
- Spelling

Prefixes

A prefix is a letter or a group of letters that comes <u>before</u> a word. The letter or letters attached to the beginning of a root word change the word's meaning.

Prefix	Definition	Example
a-	not	apolitical
ante-	before	antechamber
anti-	against	antibody
arch-	leading	archenemy
auto-	self	autograph

Prefix	Definition	Example
bi-	two	biceps
circum-	around	circumference
com-	with	community
con-	with	confront
contr-	opposing	contraband
de-	removal of	deforest
dis-	reversal of	disappear
em- (before b,m,p)	put in	embody
en-	put in	entomb
epi-	upon	epicenter
ex-	out of, from	expatriate
for-	prohibit, not do	forbid
fore-	before	forethought
hyper-	excess, more	hypersensitive
hypo-	below, less	hypothyroidism
il- (before l)	not, in	illegal
im- (before b,m,p)	not, in	impossible
in-	not, in	inadequate
inter-	between, among	interim
intra-	within, inside	intramuscular
intro-	in, into	introspection
ir- (before r)	not, in	irrefutable
mis-	wrong, lack of	mistrust
mono-	one	monotone
non-	not	nonjudgmental
over-	excessive	overbid
para-	beside, near	parallel
per-	through	pervade
peri-	enclosing, near	peripheral
post-	after	postgraduate
pre-	before	prejudge
pro-	for	prolog, pro-labor
pseudo-	false	pseudonym
re-	again	remarry
retro-	back	retrospect
sub-	below, beneath	submerge
super-	above, over	superego
trans-	across	transoceanic
un-	not	uncomfortable

When prefixes are added, the spelling of the root word does not change:

en + *able* = **enable**   *re* + *marry* = **remarry**
only the meaning changes:

Positive Meaning	Prefix	Negative Meaning
ability	in-	inability
applicable	in-	inapplicable
capable	in-	incapable
academic	non-	nonacademic
biological	non-	nonbiological
carbonated	non-	noncarbonated
creative	un-	uncreative
critical	un-	uncritical
crowded	un-	uncrowded

Suffixes

A suffix is a letter or a group of letters that comes <u>after</u> a word. The letter or letters attached to the end of a root word often change the word's meaning.

Suffix	Definition	Example
-able (-ible)	capable of	knowledgeable
-age	process, condition	pilgrimage
-al	related to	conditional
-an (-ean, -ian)	belonging to	American
-ance (-ancy,-ence)	condition	resemblance
-ary (-ery, -ory)	of	missionary
-cy	condition	residency
-dom	condition, office	kingdom
-ed	past tense	visited
-ee	recipient of	mortgagee
-en	become	darken
-er	comparative	darker
-er (-or)	person or thing	teacher
-ese	language, origin	Chinese, Taiwanese
-ess	female	goddess, waitress
-est	superlative, most	darkest
-ful	full of	useful
-hood	state of	manhood
-ic (-ical)	of, relating to	periodic
-ine	of, relating to	feline
-ing	result of	wedding
-ing (present participle)	occurring	walking
-ion (-ation, -sion)	process of	formation
-ish	of, belonging to	English, foolish
-ism	process, system	Catholicism
-ist	person who	cellist
-ite	native, follower of	Wisconsinite
-itis	inflammation	bursitis
-ity	state of	promiscuity
-ive	having tendency	productive
-ize (-ise British)	to cause,to become	hypnotize

Suffix	Definition	Example
-less	lacking	childless
-let	small, lesser	bracelet, pamphlet
-like	resembling	childlike
-log (-logue British)	speech	dialog
-logy (-ology)	science of	mineralogy
-ly	in manner of	similarly
-ment	condition of	contentment
-most	superlative, most	furthermost
-ness	condition of	wilderness
-or (-our British)	person doing verb	creator
-ous	full of	contemptuous
-ship	condition of	stewardship
-some	characterized by	loathsome
-ure	process of	indenture
-wards (-ward)	direction of	backwards, leeward
-wise	direction of	counterclockwise
-y (-ey)	characterized by	windy

When suffixes are added, the spellings sometimes change:

stop + *ed* = stopped   *ready* + *ly* = readily

the meanings always change:

Word	Positive Meaning	Negative Meaning
child	childlike	childless
contempt	◆	contemptible
rest	restful	restless
virtue	virtuous	◆
worry	◆	worrisome
worth	worthy	worthless

Spelling
and HOW TO AVOID SPELLING ERRORS

Following are the more useful spelling rules. These rules will help you spell most words correctly. Unfortunately the English language has almost as many exceptions as rules themselves. When in doubt, refer to the dictionary.

THE FINAL E

Omit the final e before adding a suffix that begins with a vowel (a, e, i, o, u):

believe + *ing* = **believing**   *corroborate* + *ive* = **corroborative**

Keep the final e before a or o if c or g precedes it.

notice + able = **noticeable**

Keep the final e before adding a suffix that begins with a consonant (usually):

bare + ly = **barely**   BUT   *true + ly* = **truly** (*not* truely)

EXERCISE FOR THE FINAL E

Change the spelling as necessary to add the suffixes:

1.   leave   -ing   _____

2.   sneeze   -ing   _____

3.   preferable   -ly   _____

4.   share   -ing   _____

5.   cure   -able   _____

DOUBLING FINAL CONSONANTS

Sometimes the last consonant of a word is doubled:

- One-syllable words: spar + ing = sparring
- Words accented on last syllable: regret + ing = regretting

EXERCISE FOR DOUBLING FINAL CONSONANTS

Change the spelling as necessary to add the suffixes:

1.   cure   -ing   _____

2.   debrief   -ing   _____

3.   get   -ing   _____

4.   meet   -ing   _____

5.   trap   -ing   _____

THE FINAL Y

Keep the final y when it is preceded by a vowel:

employ + ees = **employees**

Replace the final y with i when it is preceded by a consonant:

noisy + ly = **noisily**

PLURALS

Nouns can be made plural in many ways:
Ordinary nouns are made plural by adding s:

dog, dogs   *floor, floors*

Nouns ending in s, ch, sh, and x require an es:

fox, foxes   *sex, sexes*

Plural nouns ending in y that follow a consonant require two things:

1. The y changes to an i

2. Add an es

penny: penn + i + es = **pennies**
doily: doil + i + es = **doilies**

Plural nouns ending in y that follow a vowel (a, e, i, o, u) require an s.

attorney, attorneys

Plural nouns ending in f or fe may be formed in two ways:

1. Usually an s is added:

belief, beliefs

2. Sometimes the f is changed to v. (Then s or es is added.)

half: hal + v + es = **halves**

Plural nouns ending in o that follow a vowel (a, e, i, o, u) require an s.

stereo, stereos

Plural nouns ending in o that follow a consonant require es.

tomato, tomatoes

Plural nouns ending in o and referring to music require an s.

solo, solos

Plural letters and numbers require an apostrophe and an s.

Don't forget to dot the i's.
There are six 5's in your phone number.

Some nouns defy convention.

child,	*children*
louse,	*lice*
Mr. (Mister),	*Messrs.*
Mrs. (Mistress),	*Mmes.*
ox,	*oxen*
woman,	*women*

Other nouns remain the same, whether plural or singular.

news,	*news*
Japanese,	*Japanese*

Plural nouns that are compound (having several words) require an s̲ added to the primary noun, not the modifiers.

sister-in-law,	*sisters̲-in-law*

Foreign words create plurals in numerous ways:

addendum,	*addenda*	u̲m̲ *to* a̲
alumna,	*alumnae (feminine)*	a̲ *to* a̲e̲
alumnus,	*alumni (masculine)*	u̲s̲ *to* i̲
analysis,	*analyses*	s̲i̲s̲ *to* s̲e̲s̲
criterion,	*criteria*	o̲n̲ *to* a̲

IE and EI:
WHAT'S THE DIFFERENCE?

The rule is: i̲ before e̲, except after c̲ and the sound of a̲, as in neighbor and weigh.

However, there are many exceptions to this rule, so refer to the dictionary to be sure.

These follow rules:	These do not follow rules:
conceit, retrieve, grievance	*neither, seizure*

EXERCISE FOR IE AND EI

Add the proper letters, either ie or ei, to these words:

1. ach—ve   _____

2. fr—nd   _____

3. for—gn   _____

4. n—ce   _____

5. w—rd   _____

AMERICAN ENGLISH AND BRITISH ENGLISH: WHAT'S THE DIFFERENCE?

SPELLING

To be consistent in your word usage, it's important to use the preferred American spellings of words, rather than the British. Although British spellings are not incorrect, they are considered the <u>secondary</u> spelling for words and, as such, are inappropriate for the American style of writing. Following are examples of American and British spellings:

ILLUSTRATIONS	AMERICAN	BRITISH
-af vs. -augh	Draft	Draught
-ction vs. -xion	Retroflection	Retroflexion
-e vs. -ae	Encyclopedia	Encyclopaedia
-e excluded	Judgment	Judgement
-er vs. -re	Theater	Theatre
-et vs. -ette	Omelet	Omelette
im- vs. em-	Impanel	Empanel
in- vs. em-	Incrust	Encrust
-ize vs. -ise	Realize	Realise
-l vs. -ll	Impaneled	Empanelled
-log vs. -logue	Catalog	Catalogue
-o vs. -ou	Molding	Moulding
-or vs. -our	Favorable	Favourable

PARTS AND PARCELS OF SPEECH

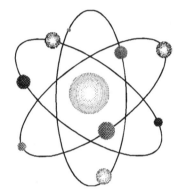

9

Although sentences are composed of subjects and predicates, these subjects and predicates are further divided into parts of speech, the same way atoms are made up of electrons, neutrons, and protons. Following is a helpful guide to the various building blocks of a sentence, the parts of speech:

- Nouns
- Pronouns
- Adjectives
- Verbs
- Adverbs
- Prepositions
- Conjunctions
- Interjections

NOUNS
or WHAT'S IN A NAME?

Nouns are words that name persons, places, things, or ideas. Because they identify various things, nouns have different classifications:

- Proper nouns
- Common nouns
- Concrete nouns
- Abstract nouns
- Collective nouns

PROPER NOUNS

Proper nouns are the names of PARTICULAR people, places, or things. Proper nouns are always capitalized:

Peter   *Asia*   *United Nations*

COMMON NOUNS

Common nouns are the names of general people, places, or things. Common nouns are not capitalized:

person   *continent*   *organization*

CONCRETE NOUNS

Concrete nouns are the names of things which can be perceived by the five senses:

SEEN   —   *sunrise*

HEARD   —   *symphony*

TOUCHED   —   *silk*

TASTED   —   *salt*

SMELLED   —   *smoke*

Concrete nouns can be general or specific. General nouns do not clearly describe your ideas. Whenever possible, use the most specific nouns you can:

General	Specific	Most Specific
clothing	*skirt*	*sarong*
medicine	*herbs*	*ginseng*

ABSTRACT NOUNS

Abstract nouns are the names of ideas or qualities. These things are intangible and cannot be experienced by the five senses:

charity   *beauty*   *trust*

Abstract nouns are very subjective. Each person has a different opinion of the ideas and the extent of the qualities. To avoid confusing your readers, use concrete nouns in place of abstract nouns:

Abstract—*He was handsome.*

Concrete—*The man's dark hair, curling around his ears and fringing the classic features of his bronzed face, set off his large, almond-shaped eyes.*

RULE NUMBER ONE: MAKE YOUR WRITING CLEAR!

COLLECTIVE NOUNS

Collective nouns are the names of groups:

department	*team*	*class*

THE CASE FOR PRONOUNS

Pronouns are nicknames for nouns. Instead of always referring to the proper name of your subject, it is easier to use a pronoun. However, if you use one incorrectly, it confuses the reader. Just decide whether the pronoun is the subject or object of the sentence, or if it shows possession, and then use its proper form.

Pronouns are easy to use with only three case forms:

- Nominative — Pronoun acts as <u>subject</u>
- Objective — Pronoun acts as <u>object</u>
- Possessive — Pronoun <u>possesses</u> (owns) something

Nominative

SUBJECT

Nominative pronouns are used as the subjects of sentences.

	Singular	Plural
1st Person	*I*	*We*
2nd Person	*You*	*You*
3rd Person	*He, She, It*	*They*

First, Second, or Third Person refers to the changing forms of the Personal Pronouns:

| 1st Person | — | The person **talking**. |
| | | *I saw Peter.* |

| 2nd Person | — | The person being **talked to**. |
| | | *You saw Peter.* |

| 3rd Person | — | The person being **talked about**. |
| | | *She saw Peter.* |

Objective

OBJECT

Objective pronouns are used as the objects of sentences.

	Singular	Plural
1st Person	*Me*	*Us*
2nd Person	*You*	*You*
3rd Person	*Him, Her, It*	*Them*

| 1st Person | — | The person **talking**. |
| | | *Jack saw me.* |

| 2nd Person | — | The person being **talked to**. |
| | | *Jack saw you.* |

| 3rd Person | — | The person being **talked about**. |
| | | *Jack saw her.* |

Possessive

OWNERSHIP

Possessive pronouns possess or own something.

	Singular	**Plural**
1st Person	*My, Mine*	*Our, Ours*
2nd Person	*Your, Yours*	*Your, Yours*
3rd Person	*His, Her(s), Its*	*Their, Theirs*

1st —	Singular	— *It is my book.*	*It is mine.*
1st —	Plural	— *It is our book.*	*It is ours.*
2nd —	Singular	— *It is your book.*	*It is yours.*
2nd —	Plural	— *It is your book.*	*It is yours.*
3rd —	Singular	— *It is her book.*	*It is hers.*
3rd —	Plural	— *It is their book.*	*It is theirs.*

Who and Whom

Who, whom, whoever, and whomever are interrogative pronouns when they are used to ask questions; they are not considered personal pronouns.

Nominative	**Objective**	**Possessive**
Who	*Whom*	*Whose* —(*not* Who's)
Whoever	*Whomever*	*Whosever*

Who *went to the store?*
You went to the store with **whom**?
Whose *store is it?*

Be careful of confusing whose, the possessive, with who's, the contraction of who is.

ADJECTIVES

Adjectives are words that define nouns and pronouns. They explain or describe the nouns more precisely. Adjectives let you express your EXACT meanings after you choose the most specific, concrete nouns possible. They modify nouns in three ways:

1.   Description   —   What kind of noun:

the _red_ balloon   the _big_ balloon

Many adjectives can be compared:

Root	Comparative	Superlative
big	bigger	biggest
beautiful	more beautiful	most beautiful
good	better	best

2.   Qualification   —   Which noun:
that balloon   _this_ balloon

3.   Limitation   —   How many nouns:
three balloons   _few_ balloons

DO NOT REPLACE concrete, specific nouns with adjectives. Instead, use the strongest nouns you can, and then further describe those nouns with adjectives.

Poor   — _The old, dilapidated, unpainted furniture was dusty._

Better — _The antiques were dusty._

Adjectives as Pronouns

Some words may be used for several purposes. Shortcuts are often taken in the English language, and this is one example of that. Here the adjective takes the place of the noun it is modifying:

Adjective   _Which apple is ripe?_

(Which defines the noun apple.)

Pronoun   _Which is ripe?_

(Which takes the place of the noun apple.)

Adjectives Used as Pronouns

all	another	any	both
each	either	few	many
more	most	much	neither
one	other	several	some
that	these	this	those
what	which		

LIGHTS, CAMERAS, VERBS!

Action and verbs are the same. Verbs are words that express action or make a statement. Because of this, verbs deliver power. They make the difference between weak writing and forceful writing. To express yourself forcefully, use strong verbs.

Use Strong Verbs

Don't weaken verbs by using helping verbs <u>can</u>, <u>could</u>, <u>might</u>, <u>may</u>.

Write with authority.
Express yourself.
Drive your points home.

Notice how much more credible the strong verbs are than these:

You <u>may</u> write with authority.
You <u>could</u> express yourself.
You <u>might</u> drive your points home.

Verbs and Time

In addition to using strong verbs, be sure to use the proper tenses of verbs. In this way, you can keep your reader informed of TIME.

There are basically two tenses, present and past, but with the help of auxiliary verbs, you can inform your reader of the future, the present perfect, the past perfect, and the future perfect. With the aid of -<u>ing</u>, you can inform your reader of a continuous action.

- Present Tense
- Past Tense
- Future Tense
- Present Perfect Tense
- Past Perfect Tense
- Future Perfect Tense
- Progressive Tenses

Present Tense

By using the present tense, your reader understands that something is happening NOW:

Present time	—	*I see the cat.*
Habitual time	—	*I see the cat every afternoon.*
Historical present	—	*Scarlett O'Hara sees the plantation.*
Literary present	—	*In Gone With the Wind, Margaret Mitchell prepares Scarlett for the future.*
Future action	—	*The bill goes before Congress tomorrow.*

> In the present tense, remember the third person singular needs an -s ending for the verb:

	Singular	Plural
1st person	*I see*	*We see*
2nd person	*You see*	*You see*
3rd person	*He sees*	*They see*
	She sees	
	It sees	

Past Tense

By using the past tense, your reader understands that something has already happened in the PAST. For regular verbs, add a -d or -ed ending to the present tense of the verb:

Present	Past
look	*looked*
sneeze	*sneezed*

Problems don't develop with the past tense until you come to the irregular verbs. These use peculiar means to form the past tense. Always check your dictionary when in doubt, but following is a list of the more troublesome irregular verbs.

IRREGULAR VERBS

Present	Past	Past Participle	
awake	awoke	(have)	awoke
bear	bore	"	borne
beat	beat	"	beaten
become	became	"	become
begin	began	"	begun
bend	bent	"	bent
bid (offer price)	bid	"	bid
bid (give order)	bade (bid)	"	bidden (bid)
bite	bit	"	bitten
bleed	bled	"	bled
blow	blew	"	blown
break	broke	"	broken
bring	brought	"	brought
build	built	"	built
burst	burst	"	burst
buy	bought	"	bought
catch	caught	"	caught
choose	chose	"	chosen
come	came	"	come
creep	crept	"	crept
cut	cut	"	cut
deal	dealt	"	dealt
dig	dug	"	dug
dive	dived (dove)	"	dived
do	did	"	done
drag	dragged	"	dragged
draw	drew	"	drawn
drink	drank	"	drunk
drive	drove	"	driven
drown	drowned	"	drowned
eat	ate	"	eaten
fall	fell	"	fallen
fight	fought	"	fought
flee	fled	"	fled
fling	flung	"	flung
fly	flew	"	flown
forget	forgot	"	forgotten (forgot)
freeze	froze	"	frozen
get	got	"	gotten (got)
give	gave	"	given
go	went	"	gone
grow	grew	"	grown
hang (a criminal)	hanged	"	hanged
hang (a picture)	hung	"	hung
have	had	"	had
hide	hid	"	hidden
hold	held	"	held

Present	Past	Past Participle
hurt	hurt	(have) hurt
keep	kept	" kept
know	knew	" known
lay (to put)	laid	" laid
lead	led	" led
leave	left	" left
lend	lent	" lent
let	let	" let
lie (to rest)	lay	" lain
lie (an untruth)	lied	" lied
lose	lost	" lost
mean	meant	" meant
prove	proved	" proved (proven)
raise	raised	" raised
read	read	" read
ride	rode	" ridden
ring	rang	" rung
rise	rose	" risen
run	ran	" run
say	said	" said
see	saw	" seen
sell	sold	" sold
send	sent	" sent
set	set	" set
sew	sewed	" sewed (sewn)
shake	shook	" shaken
shave	shaved	" shaved (shaven)
shine (give light)	shone	" shone
shine (polish)	shined	" shined
shrink	shrank (shrunk)	" shrunk
show	showed	" showed (shown)
sing	sang (sung)	" sung
sink	sank (sunk)	" sunk
sit	sat	" sat
slay	slew	" slain
speak	spoke	" spoken
spring	sprang (sprung)	" sprung
steal	stole	" stolen
sting	stung	" stung
swear	swore	" sworn
swim	swam	" swum
swing	swung	" swung
take	took	" taken
teach	taught	" taught
tear	tore	" torn
tell	told	" told
think	thought	" thought
throw	threw	" thrown
wear	wore	" worn

Present	Past	Past Participle
win	won	(have) won
write	wrote	" written

Some of these irregular verbs are especially tricky:

Present		Past	Past	Participle	
lie	(to rest)	lay	(have)	lain	INTRANSITIVE
lay	(to put)	laid	"	laid	TRANSITIVE
sit	(to rest)	sat	"	sat	INTRANSITIVE
set	(to put)	set	"	set	TRANSITIVE
rise	(to go up)	rose	"	risen	INTRANSITIVE
raise	(to cause to go up)	raised	"	raised	TRANSITIVE

Verbs can be transitive or intransitive:

Transitive verbs take an object. Intransitive verbs do not.

Here's a trick to remembering:

Transitive sounds like transport: it transports some object.

Transitive	*— I lay the book on the table.*	Object —	*the book*
Intransitive	*— I lie down often.*	NO Object	
Transitive	*— I set the book on the desk.*	Object —	*the book*
Intransitive	*— I sit down often.*	NO Object	
Transitive	*— I raise the flag in parades.*	Object —	*the flag*
Intransitive	*— I rise every morning.*	NO Object	

Future Tense

By using the future tense, your reader understands that something will happen in the FUTURE. To form the future tense, use shall or will before the verb:

> *I shall see.*
> *You will see.*

Present Perfect Tense

By using the present perfect tense, your reader understands that something occurred in the recent past or that something began in the past and continues into the present. To form the present perfect tense, use <u>have</u> or <u>has</u> before the verb:

I have washed the car every week this year.

You have washed the car every week this year.

*He **HAS** washed the car every week this year.*

*She **HAS** washed the car every week this year.*

*It **HAS** washed the car every week this year.*

We have washed the car every week this year.

You have washed the car every week this year.

They have washed the car every week this year.

Third person singular uses _HAS_, while all others use _HAVE_.

Past Perfect Tense

By using the past perfect tense, your reader understands that something HAS ALREADY occurred BEFORE some other event. To form the past perfect tense, use <u>had</u> before the verb:

He <u>had</u> washed the car before he left.

Future Perfect Tense

By using the future perfect tense, your reader understands that something WILL occur in the future BEFORE some other event. To form the future perfect tense, use <u>will have</u> before the verb:

He <u>will have</u> washed the car before he leaves.

Progressive Tenses

By using the progressive form of a tense, your reader understands that some action IS CONTINUING. All six tenses have a progressive form. To make the progressive forms, add a helping verb and -ing to the main verb:

Present Progressive	—	*I am speaking.*
Past Progressive	—	*I was speaking.*
Future Progressive	—	*I shall be speaking.*
Future Progressive	—	*She will be speaking.*
Present Perfect Progressive	—	*I have been speaking.*
Present Perfect Progressive	—	*He has been speaking.*
Past Perfect Progressive	—	*I had been speaking.*
Future Perfect Progressive	—	*I shall have been speaking.*
Future Perfect Progressive	—	*You will have been speaking.*

Active and Passive Voice

Energetic writing uses the active voice. Vague, boring writing uses the passive voice. Except for certain instances, always use the active voice; it will keep your readers interested and awake.

The active voice describes an action done BY its subject.
The passive voice describes an action done TO its subject.

Active	—	*She wrote the report.*
Passive	—	*The report was written.*
Passive	—	*The report was written by her.*

The passive voice is useful when you WANT the writing to appear vague.

Passive— *A salary cut was proposed.*   VAGUE, NONACCUSATORY
Active — *Mr. Jones proposed a salary cut.* CLEAR, ACCUSATORY

Passive verbs *may* or *may not* use a "by phrase" to tell who performed the action:

To stress the performer, use the "by phrase."

Land is bought BY Peter.

To stress the subject, use the "by phrase."

Land is bought BY Peter.
Gold is bought BY William.

To conceal performer's name, do NOT use the "by phrase."

> *The property was bought.* (by land speculators)
> *A salary cut was proposed.* (by Mr. Jones)

To avoid responsibility, do NOT use the "by phrase."

> *A glass was broken.* (by me)
> *An error was made.* (by the manager)

When performer isn't important or isn't known, do NOT use the "by phrase."

> *Land is bought everyday.* (by someone)

To mimic scientific terminology, do NOT use the "by phrase."

> *A black hole is formed in the vacuum of space.*
> (by a collapsed star)
>
> *XYZ pain reliever has been widely prescribed.*
> (by doctors)

Used in small amounts, the passive voice adds variety to your writing. As an adjective, the passive voice is sometimes preferred.

PASSIVE VERBS USED AS ADJECTIVES

Past participles can describe a noun passively.

> *A woman was shocked by the typhoon.*
> *OR*
> *She was a **shocked** woman.*

> *A man was tired by the heavy load.*
> *OR*
> *He was a **tired** man.*

Past participles can describe a present condition caused by an action in the past.

> *John broke the clock yesterday.*
> *OR*
> *The clock **is broken**.*

> *I tore my sleeve this morning.*
> *OR*
> *My sleeve **is torn**.*

An active verb's object is a passive verb's subject.
Passive = BE + past participle.

ACTIVE			PASSIVE		
Peter	*buys*	*land.*	*Land*	*is bought*	*by Peter.*
Peter	*is buying*	*land.*	*Land*	*is being bought*	*by Peter.*
Peter	*has bought*	*land.*	*Land*	*has been bought*	*by Peter.*
Peter	*bought*	*land.*	*Land*	*was bought*	*by Peter.*
Peter	*was buying*	*land.*	*Land*	*was being bought*	*by Peter.*
Peter	*had bought*	*land.*	*Land*	*had been bought*	*by Peter.*
Peter	*will buy*	*land.*	*Land*	*will be bought*	*by Peter.*
Peter	*is going to buy*	*land.*	*Land*	*is going to be bought*	*by Peter.*
Peter	*will have bought*	*land.*	*Land*	*will have been bought*	*by Peter.*

PASSIVE FORM OF MODALS

Passive = modal + BE + past participle.

William	**can**	be	promoted	in the department.
William	**had better**	be	promoted	as soon as possible.
William	**must**	be	promoted	without delay.
William	**should**	be	promoted	after the holiday.
William	**ought to**	be	promoted	ahead of schedule.
William	**shall**	be	promoted	from clerk.

Past-Passive = modal + HAVE BEEN + past participle.

William	**could**	have been	promoted	to vice presidency.
William	**might**	have been	promoted	before January.
William	**may**	have been	promoted	within the company.
William	**will**	have been	promoted	at the meeting.
William	**would**	have been	promoted	from the ranks.

RULE OF THUMB: Avoid using the passive voice; however, there are exceptions.

For more information about the times you WANT the writing to appear vague, see the **PASSIVE VOICE (IN MODERATION)** segment of the **REPORTS' TONE: LEVELS OF FORMALITY** section. **CHAPTER 17**

ADVERBS

Adverbs are words used to describe <u>how</u>, <u>how much</u>, <u>how often</u>, <u>when</u>, and <u>where</u>.

HOW	He sings	beautifully.
HOW MUCH	He sings	long.
HOW OFTEN	He sings	regularly.
WHEN	He sings	soon.
WHERE	He sings	here.

Adverbs define verbs, adjectives, and other adverbs.

Adverbs modify verbs:

She dances <u>gracefully</u>.

Adverbs modify adjectives:

The garden was <u>surprisingly</u> large.

Adverbs modify other adverbs:

They studied <u>very</u> regularly.

PREPOSITIONS

Prepositions are structure words that show the relationship between a noun or pronoun and another word in the sentence. Prepositions always introduce phrases. The objects of the phrases are nouns or pronouns that appear at the ends of the phrases.

The store <u>down</u> the road sells shoes.

down	is the preposition
road	is the object of the preposition
down the road	is the prepositional phrase
store and road	are the two nouns that are related

Prepositions

about	above	across	after
against	along	amid	amidst
among	amongst	around	aside from
at	before	behind	below
beneath	beside(s)	between	beyond
but (all but)	by	concerning	down
during	except	for	from
in	in spite of	into	like
of	off	on	on account of
over	past	since	through
throughout	to	toward	under
underneath	until	unto	up
upon	with	within	without
with regard to			

EXERCISE FOR TIME: PREPOSITION

Arrange the following time words into the correct columns.

Examples:

I'll see you   <u>at</u> 5:00 <u>on</u> Wednesday <u>in</u> September

RULES OF THUMB

AT	—	For shortest spans of time use <u>at</u>.
AT	—	For specific occasions use <u>at</u>.
ON	—	For medium spans of time use <u>on</u>.
IN	—	For longest spans of time use <u>in</u>.

April	Tuesday	7 o'clock	noon
summer	Christmas	1994	6:20
Sunday	Monday evening	five minutes	1856
2004	the morning	the first	Friday
autumn	quarter past two	half past one	midnight

AT	ON	IN
_____	_____	_____
_____	_____	_____
_____	_____	_____
_____	_____	_____
_____	_____	_____
_____	_____	_____
_____	_____	_____

CONJUNCTIONS

Conjunctions are structure words that connect words and groups of words. There are three kinds of conjunctions:

1. Coordinating conjunctions
2. Correlative conjunctions
3. Subordinating conjunctions

COORDINATING CONJUNCTIONS

Coordinating conjunctions join words, clauses, or phrases of the same grammatical type. The following words are coordinating conjunctions:

and		but		or	
	nor		for		yet

Coordinating conjunctions join words:

NOUNS	The _cat_ and _dog_ played
VERBS	They _played_ and _fought_.
ADVERBS	They fought _hard_ and _long_.

Coordinating conjunctions join clauses:

DEPENDENT CLAUSES   *They played <u>when they wanted</u> and <u>when they didn't</u>.*

INDEPENDENT CLAUSES *<u>The cat played</u>, but <u>the dog didn't play</u>.*

Independent clauses joined by a coordinating conjunction require a comma before the conjunction:

She was promoted<u>, and</u> he was demoted.

He worked overtime<u>, but</u> she went home.

Coordinating conjunctions join phrases:

PREPOSITIONAL PHRASE *They play before breakfast, after lunch, and in the evening.*

CORRELATIVE CONJUNCTIONS

Correlative conjunctions are used in sets. The following words are correlative conjunctions:

both...and	*either...or*	*neither...nor*
not only...but	*whether...or*	

<u>Either</u> the dog <u>or</u> the cat must go out.

<u>Both</u> William <u>and</u> John are going to the concert.

SUBORDINATING CONJUNCTIONS

Subordinating conjunctions are often called adverbial subordinating conjunctions because they usually begin adverb clauses. These join dependent clauses to independent clauses:

Don't call me <u>before</u> I'm done eating.

before	**conjunction**
before I'm done eating	**dependent clause**

They wanted to finish <u>because</u> they were late.

because	**conjunction**
because they were late	**dependent clause**

Subordinating Conjunctions

after	although	as	as much as
because	before	how	if
in order that	provided	since	so that
that	than	though	till
unless	until	when	whenever
where	wherever	while	

INTERJECTIONS

Interjections are words which express emotion.

Sentence interjections may be punctuated as sentences:

Oh! Good Heavens! Ouch! No! Yeah!

Interjections may also be incorporated into sentences. In that case, they are set off by commas and have no relation to other words in those sentences:

Oh, don't just stand there! No, I said I don't want any!

SENTENCES

10

AND THEIR CRAFTSMANSHIP

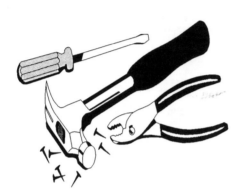

A sentence is a group of words that expresses your thoughts. Your reason for writing the sentence is its purpose, and the arrangement of your words is its composition.

HOW you write or *craft* your sentence is what determines your business style. As a result, good sentence craftsmanship is one of the most important aspects of your business writing.

Sentence Crafting includes six main areas:

1. Purpose
2. Composition
3. Classification
4. Sentence Errors
   - Fragments
   - Run-on Sentences
5. Agreement
   - Agreement of Pronouns
   - Agreement of Verbs
6. Collective Nouns

PURPOSE

Why you form this sentence classifies it into one of four kinds.

Kinds of Sentences

Declarative—states—(Most common kind of sentence)
I want the red shirt.

Imperative—commands or requests—(*You* is the implied subject)
Give me the red shirt. (You give me the red shirt.)

Interrogative—asks—?
Do you have a red shirt?

Exclamatory—exclaims— !
You do have a red shirt!

COMPOSITION

A sentence is composed of two parts:

- Subject—*Who* or *what* the sentence describes
- Predicate—What the subject *did* or what *happened*

Subject

A *simple* subject is a word (or words) which names the following:

- person
- place
- thing
- idea

A *compound* subject is two (or more) *connected* naming words; often the connecting words are these:

- and—dogs and cats
- or—dogs or cats

A subject is the word (or words) which tells *who* or *what*.

A predicate is the word (or group of words) which tells what the subject *did* or what *happened*.

Predicate

A *simple* predicate (or VERB) is the word (or words) which describes the action of the sentence.

Sentence	*The dog wagged his tail.*
Predicate	*wagged his tail*
Simple Predicate—VERB	*wagged*

A *compound verb* is two (or more) connected verbs.

Sentence	*The dog whined and wagged his tail.*
Predicate	*whined and wagged his tail*
Simple Predicate—COMPOUND VERB	*whined and wagged*

CLASSIFICATION

How you build a sentence determines its structure.

Classification of Sentences:

SIMPLE SENTENCE

- One Main Clause
- No Dependent Clauses

The dog chased the cat.

COMPOUND SENTENCE

- Two (or more) Main Clauses
- No Dependent Clauses

The dog chased the cat, and the cat chased the dog.

COMPLEX SENTENCE

- One Main Clause
- One (or more) Dependent Clauses

After the dog chased the cat, the cat chased the dog.

   After the dog chased the cat—is the dependent clause

COMPOUND-COMPLEX SENTENCE

- Two (or more) Main Clauses
- One (or more) Dependent Clauses

The dog chased the cat, which had been sleeping, and the cat chased the dog.

which had been sleeping—is the dependent clause

Variety for Effect

Variety, as they say, is the spice of life. It's also the zest of writing. Vary your sentence structures; include the different kinds of sentences. These make your reports and proposals more entertaining. If the sentences are all alike, the reading becomes dull. If your audience is bored, it will lose interest.

Monotony Hypnotizes

Mix long and short sentences. Change the word order occasionally. Insert a dependent clause at the beginning, middle, and end of sentences. Vary your sentence structures. You don't want to hypnotize your audience the way an unbroken white line in the center of a highway hypnotizes drivers.

SENTENCE ERRORS

A sentence is a COMPLETE thought.
A sentence error can occur in one of two ways:

- Fragment—only *part* of a sentence or thought
- Run-on—*two* sentences or thoughts joined incorrectly

Fragments

A sentence is a group of words composed of three elements; it is a complete thought which contains a subject and verb.

- Complete thought
- Subject
- Verb (predicate)

**If a group of words lacks any one of these, it is a fragment.
A fragment is an incomplete thought or a partial sentence.**

EXAMPLE 1:

The dog chasing the cat.—**Fragment—lacks a verb**

chasing needs a helping verb

TO CORRECT THIS ERROR, USE A HELPING VERB.

The dog IS chasing the cat.—**Corrected**

A verb phrase is formed from a main verb and a helping verb.

Helping Verbs

am	are	be
is	can	can be
can have	could	could be
could have	have	has
had (been)	have been	has been
will have been	may	may have
may have been	might	might have
might have been	must	must have
must have been	shall	shall have
shall have been	should	should have
should have been	will	will have
will have been	would	would have
would have been		

EXAMPLE 2:

In the front yard I saw the dog. Chasing the cat.—**Fragment**

TO CORRECT THIS ERROR, COMBINE THE FIRST SENTENCE WITH THE PARTICIPIAL PHRASE.

In the front yard I saw the dog chasing the cat.—**Corrected**

EXAMPLE 3:

The dog chased the animal. A cat.—**Fragment**

TO CORRECT THIS ERROR, COMBINE THE FIRST SENTENCE WITH THE APPOSITIVE (THE EXPLANATION) OF THE SECOND. USE A COMMA TO SET OFF AN APPOSITIVE.

The dog chased the animal, a cat.—**Corrected**

EXAMPLE 4:

When the dog chased the cat. The cat chased the dog.

TO CORRECT THIS ERROR, COMBINE THE FIRST DEPENDENT CLAUSE WITH THE SECOND INDEPENDENT CLAUSE. USE A COMMA.

When the dog chased the cat, the cat chased the dog.—**Corrected**

Do not separate a phrase, an appositive, or a dependent clause from its sentence.

Run-on Sentences

A run-on sentence is the incorrect combination of two sentences. It can occur in two ways:

- Comma splice
- No punctuation

COMMA SPLICE

A comma splice occurs when two sentences are joined with a comma which has no coordinator. Coordinators, also called coordinating conjunctions, are the words <u>and</u>, <u>but</u>, <u>or</u>, <u>nor</u>, <u>for</u>, and <u>yet</u>.

The dog chased the cat, the cat chased the dog.

TO CORRECT THIS ERROR, USE A COORDINATOR WITH THE COMMA.

The dog chased the cat, <u>and</u> the cat chased the dog.—**Corrected**

There are three ways to repair comma-splice sentences:

1. Comma and coordinator
2. Semicolon (and no coordinator)
3. Periods for both sentences

    1. The dog chased the cat, and the cat chased the dog.
    Use a coordinator with the comma.

    2. The dog chased the cat; the cat chased the dog.
    Use a semicolon (and no coordinator).

    3. The dog chased the cat. The cat chased the dog.
    Use a period for each of the two sentences.

NO PUNCTUATION

The dog chased the cat the cat chased the dog.

TO CORRECT THIS ERROR, USE ONE OF THE THREE METHODS OF REPAIRING SENTENCES:

1. Comma and coordinator
2. Semicolon (and no coordinator)
3. Periods for both sentences

    1. The dog chased the cat, and the cat chased the dog.
      Use a coordinator with the comma.

    2. The dog chased the cat; the cat chased the dog.
      Use a semicolon (and no coordinator).

    3. The dog chased the cat. The cat chased the dog.
      Use a period for each of the two sentences.

AGREEMENT

For sentences to be correct, the subject and verb must agree in number. When a subject is singular, it must have a singular verb; when a subject is plural, it must have a plural verb.

Singular	—	*The dog is chasing the cat.*
Plural	—	*The dogs are chasing the cat.*
Singular	—	*The child is chasing the dog.*
Plural	—	*The children are chasing the dog.*
Singular	—	*The boy goes to school.*
Plural	—	*The boys go to school.*

Most verbs ending in s̲ are singular:

    She is, was, has, does, wants, sees, touches.

Most verbs in the present tense *not* ending in s̲ are plural:

    They are, were, have, do, want, see, touch.

Don't be fooled by prepositional phrases. If the subject is singular, the verb should also be singular. Don't pay attention to the number in the prepositional phrase. In fact, mentally ~~cross out~~ prepositional phrases, so you can see the subject and verb more clearly.

> The number ~~of the teams~~ was two.
> The number was two.
>
> The ride ~~through the mountains~~ was exciting.
> The ride was exciting.

Find your subject and verb—and the rest will follow. Prepositional phrases only confuse the issue, so find the subject to learn whether it's singular or plural; then you can choose your verb accordingly.

Agreement of Pronouns

Be careful of pronouns and their agreement with verbs.

Singular pronouns:

anyone	each	either
everybody	everyone	neither
nobody	no one	one
somebody	someone	

> Anyone is eligible.
> Anyone of the contestants is eligible.
> Everybody wants to win.
> Everybody in all the departments wants to win.

The words every or many a, if appearing before a noun (or nouns), require a singular verb.

> Every Tom, Dick, and Harry is eligible.
> Many a girl has caught his eye.

SINGULAR or PLURAL PRONOUNS

Quantitative words are singular or plural depending upon the nouns they refer to:

all	any	half	most
more	part	none	some

All of the afternoon <u>was</u> sunny.
a singular quantity (afternoon)

All of the days <u>were</u> sunny.
a plural number (days)

Any of the contestants <u>is</u> eligible.
a single number (any <u>one</u> is eligible)

Any of the contestants <u>are</u> eligible.
a plural number (<u>all</u> are eligible)

Plural pronouns:

both	few	many	several

Agreement of Verbs

Watch your verbs' agreement with pronouns:

Third person singular uses **DOES/DOESN'T**.
First and second person singular use **DO/DON'T**.
First, second, and third person plural use **DO/DON'T**.

	Do—Don't	**Does—Doesn't**
Singular		
First person	*I do*	
Second person	*You don't*	
Third person		*He does*
Third person		*She doesn't*
Third person		*It does*
Plural		
First person	*We don't*	
Second person	*You do*	
Third person	*They don't*	

COMPOUND SUBJECTS

Usually when two subjects are joined by <u>and</u>, they are considered plural and require a plural verb.

> *The cat and the dog are chasing each other.*
> Subject<u>s</u>—cat and dog;   verb—are

Exception to the rule: When two subjects are considered a single unit, they require a singular verb.

> *Love and marriage is the best advice for him.*
> Subject—love and marriage; verb—is

To double-check if it is correct, reverse the words:

> *The best advice for him is love and marriage.*
> Subject—advice; verb—is

Or, either...or, nor, neither...nor

When singular subjects are joined by the words <u>or</u>, <u>either...or</u>, <u>nor</u>, or <u>neither...nor</u>, they require singular verbs.

> *Either he or she is going.*

> *Neither the cat nor the dog wants to run.*

When plural subjects are joined by the words <u>or</u>, <u>either...or</u>, <u>nor</u>, or <u>neither...nor</u>, they require plural verbs.

> *Neither his friends nor those of hers are well-known.*

The verb agrees with the nearer subject when one singular subject and one plural subject are joined by the words <u>or</u>, <u>nor</u>.

> *Neither the cat nor the dogS want to run.*
> *Neither the cats nor the dog wantS to run.*

The verb agrees with the nearer subject when the subjects differ in number (as above) or in person (as follows):

---

*Either he or I **AM** going home.*
*Either I or he **IS** going home.*

COLLECTIVE NOUNS

A collective noun is one which refers to a group as a single unit. It requires a singular verb.

army	audience	class	club
committee	company	crew	crowd
faculty	family	fleet	flock
group	herd	jury	majority
minority	squadron	swarm	troop

Depending upon its treatment, a collective noun is singular or plural.

The team has won the game.

(team is treated as a whole)

The team have won the game.

(team is treated as individuals)

Words referring to amount are usually singular:

Time	—	*Two weeks is not enough time.*
Money	—	*Twelve dollars is the total cost.*
Weight	—	*Nine pounds was the baby's weight.*
Fractions	—	*Four-fifths is a large enough majority.*
Volume	—	*Seven gallons fills the gas tank.*
Measurement	—	*Six feet is the right height.*

Titles of books and works of art are treated as singular.

Sharon Gibb's novel <u>Summer Nights</u> is my favorite book.

Some words that appear plural are singular.

civics	economics	mathematics	measles
mumps	news	physics	politics

Mathematics was my worst subject in school.

Paragraphs and Paranoia

Now that you're familiar with the **building blocks** of paragraphs
—*the words, parts of speech, and creation of sentences*—
you're ready to tackle paragraphs. Don't be afraid of them.

Paragraphs are easy!

- Paragraphs are logical expressions of ideas or key points.

- Each paragraph examines ONE idea only.

- Each paragraph has a beginning, a middle, and an end.

The beginning, middle, and end correspond with the topic sentence, supporting sentences, and concluding sentence.

This pattern is completed by a *transitional* sentence that guides the readers to the next paragraph.

Beginning	⇨	*Topic Sentence*
Middle	⇨	*Supporting Sentences*
End	⇨	*Concluding Sentence*

Transition

Paragraphs are organized into four parts for these reasons:

1. The **topic** sentence ANNOUNCES your idea.
2. The **supporting** sentences EXPLAIN it.
3. The **concluding** sentence MAKES the point, reinforces the idea.
4. The **transitional** sentence DIRECTS the readers from this paragraph's idea to the next.

TOPIC SENTENCE ⇨ Tell them what you're going to tell them

SUPPORTING SENTENCES ⇨ Tell them

CONCLUDING SENTENCE ⇨ Tell them what you told them

and

TRANSITIONAL SENTENCE ⇨ Tell them WHERE you're going next

Plan Your Thoughts

To construct a paragraph, you must first *plan* your thoughts. Consider these things:

Audience

WHO am I writing for?

- WORD choice
- READERS' objective(s)

Purpose

WHY am I writing?

- MY objective(s)

Limit

WHAT *exactly* do I want to say?

- CHOOSE *one part* of the picture

Arrange Your Thoughts—Limn or Outline Your Thoughts

After planning your thoughts, you must *arrange* your thoughts. To do this, simply write down your thoughts on a piece of paper.

You will notice two patterns forming:

    1. The Subject is...

        the list of ideas, the whole picture.

    2. Topic Sentences are...

        the best ideas, the picture's parts.

TOPIC SENTENCES

Your most important ideas become your topic sentences in this way:

    WRITE YOUR BEST IDEAS IN COMPLETE SENTENCE FORM!

Your ideas which began as a few words (or fragments of sentences) are now written as COMPLETE sentences—not as fragments. Remember, the topic sentence is USUALLY the FIRST sentence of each paragraph.

Topic sentences do three things:

- **Present** Ideas

- **Introduce** Main Topic of Each Paragraph

- **Connect** Parts

Because topic sentences are the "blueprints" for the paragraphs, they also *combine* all the elements of each paragraph. They unify the topic sentences, supporting sentences, and concluding sentences, so the parts work together as a whole to describe *one idea.*

Topic Sentences and Their Arrangement

Now *arrange* your topic sentences into a logical order.
Each topic sentence is one idea, one part of your report.
Organize the parts into a whole.

Three main categories of arrangement:

Time	⇨	*Chronological*
Space	⇨	*Spatial*
Importance	⇨	*Dynamics*

Time = Chronological

If organized by time, the topic sentences follow a chronological order of
events as they have happened or as they will happen.

In June the team suggested an experiment.

On July second they began the testing.

In August they completed the experiment.

Space = Spatial

If organized by space, the topic sentences describe the location of the
subject in relation to other subjects. Use words such as <u>beside</u>, <u>near</u>, <u>close</u>,
<u>approaching</u>, <u>remote</u>, <u>distant</u>, <u>isolated</u> to relate the topic sentences to each
other.

The keyboard is located in front of the computer.

It is beside the monitor.

The keyboard is isolated fom the electric outlet.

Importance = Dynamics

If organized by importance, the topic sentences build to a crescendo, from
the least to the most important idea.

ALWAYS END WITH A
BANG!

To convince your readers, save your best idea for last.

Our company has twelve years of experience.

We consistently produce high profits for our clients.

Our company will increase your firm's profits by 10%.

EXERCISE FOR PARAGRAPH PROGRESSION

Arrange these topic sentences in a dynamic progression, beginning from the weakest point and ending with the strongest:

Statement of Purpose—*Why you should purchase THIS stock.*

Topic Sentences:

—It gives dividends.

—It usually shows a yearly profit.

—It is underrated.

—It will split soon.

EXERCISE I FOR TOPIC SENTENCES

Write a topic sentence about each of the following subjects:

A red Ferrari sports car's performance

_____

A wedding celebration

_____

A tropical beach at sunset

_____

EXERCISE II FOR TOPIC SENTENCES

Following are several supporting sentences. Write a topic sentence for them:

Owning your home saves money because it invests the mortgage payments, instead of wasting the rental payments. Whether the stock market goes up or down, land values increase at a relatively constant rate. Currencies can spiral in value or devaluate. However, owning property is the best barrier to inflation.

SUPPORTING SENTENCES

Supporting sentences *support* your topic sentences. They prove that the idea you have introduced in that paragraph is true. Because of their specific details, they offer evidence that your idea is both logical and credible.

Supporting sentences make up the largest part of each paragraph. Although a paragraph can have only one topic sentence and one concluding sentence, it can have many supporting sentences.

EXERCISE I FOR SUPPORTING SENTENCES

Write supporting sentences about each of the following subjects. Use the topic sentences you wrote in **EXERCISE I FOR TOPIC SENTENCES**:

A red Ferrari sports car's performance

A wedding celebration

_____

_____

_____

A tropical beach at sunset

_____

_____

_____

Supporting Sentences and Unity

Supporting sentences should form a connection among these three types of sentences:

1. The topic sentence
2. The other supporting sentences
3. The concluding sentence

All the parts must work together to form a unified whole.

If any of the supporting sentences do NOT contribute to the whole, do one of two things:

1. IF WEAK   —Delete—cross out those sentences
2. IF STRONG   —Use as TOPIC sentences for NEW paragraphs

EXERCISE II FOR SUPPORTING SENTENCES

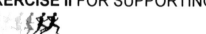

This exercise will help to demonstrate unity within a paragraph. All the parts should belong to the whole. If some parts do not belong, then the paragraph is not unified. Delete or cross out the supporting sentences that do NOT belong in the following paragraph:

A house is a home. Where you live is more than just a residence. It is a refuge to which you can escape from the problems of the world. Home is a place where loved ones offer support. Houses are good investments. A house is a retreat from the difficulties of the workplace, school, the office. Many people do not have homes of their own. Indeed, your house is much more than a place to hang your hat; it's home.

CONCLUDING SENTENCES

Every paragraph needs a concluding sentence to alert the audience that the paragraph is ending. A concluding sentence summarizes the idea of the paragraph which also helps to unify it. It restates the topic sentence, but in stronger words.

A concluding sentence does three things:

1. INFORMS   readers that paragraph is ending
2. SUMMARIZES paragraph's idea
3. RESTATES   topic sentence

A concluding sentence and a topic sentence are VERY similar. The difference is that the concluding sentence is worded more convincingly than the topic sentence.

EXERCISE FOR CONCLUDING SENTENCE

Following is a topic sentence and supporting sentences. Write a concluding sentence to complete this paragraph:

Learning to write a paragraph is easy. You need only to introduce your subject with a topic sentence. Then you write several detailed sentences to support your idea. Finally you write a concluding sentence that restates your topic sentence.

_____

_____

TRANSITIONAL SENTENCES

A transition is the final sentence in a paragraph that connects the idea of *this* paragraph to the idea of the *next* paragraph.

Transitions are like signposts that point the way for readers.

As hand gestures and facial expressions reveal what you mean when speaking, transitional sentences show what you mean when writing.

They make it easy for your readers to follow your thoughts.

Transitional sentences SHOW the readers where you're going. They indicate the progression of your ideas in six ways:

1.   To offer an example
2.   To extend a thought
3.   To limit a thought
4.   To conclude a thought
5.   To show time
6.   To show space

Example

Transitions can be used **to offer examples** with the following words and phrases:

as	for example	for instance
for this purpose	likewise	such as

For example, this book makes writing easy.

Extension

Transitions can be used **to extend thoughts** with the following words and phrases:

also	another	at last
consequently	furthermore	for this purpose
likewise	otherwise	similarly
such	then	on the other hand

Writing requires practice; ***consequently*** *this book makes writing easy.*

Limiting

Transitions can be used **to limit thoughts** with the following words and phrases:

accordingly	although	but	besides
equally important	if this be true	in fact	then
otherwise	on the other hand	such	yet
nevertheless	on the contrary	whereas	

> *Writing is hard work;* **on the other hand**, *this book makes writing easy.*

Concluding

Transitions can be used **to conclude thoughts** with the following words and phrases:

as a result	as can be seen	as shown above
consequently	for these reasons	for this reason
generally speaking	hence	in any case
in any event	in brief	in conclusion
in either case	in fact	in other words
in summary	on the whole	therefore
thus	to sum up	

> **To sum up**, *this book makes writing easy!*

Time

Transitions can be used **to show time** with the following words and phrases:

after	at the present time	at the same time
at this point	before	during
eventually	finally	first (second)
further	hence	henceforth
in time	in due time	later
meanwhile	next	once
secondly	since	sooner or later
then	until	until now
when	whenever	

> **In due time**, *this book makes writing easy.*

Space

Transitions can be used **to show space** with the following words and phrases:

above	across from	adjacent to	also
before me	below	beyond	further
nearby	here	next to	in the distance
on the left	on the right	opposite to	there
to the left	to the right	where	wherever

In front of me is this book.

The most important point about writing is to make it simple for readers to understand. SHOW THEM YOUR THOUGHTS' DIRECTION!

Remember:

Topic Sentence

Supporting Sentences

Concluding Sentence

Transitional Sentence

PARAGRAPH

PARAGRAPH FORMS

Now a word about paragraph forms: the tried and true block and indented paragraphs are not the only kinds. There are many. However, for business writing five forms are appropriate:

1. Block
2. Indented
3. Left-margin Notation
4. Numbered
5. Unique

Block Paragraphs

This is the preferred style. Using no indentations, each paragraph begins at the left margin. A blank line separates each paragraph.

Dear Ms. Wright:

Thank you for your interest in Olley Manufacturing. At this time there are no openings, but with your qualifications, you'll soon find employment.

We'll keep your resume on record for one year. Please keep in touch with us, because when hiring begins, you'll be our first choice.

Indented Paragraphs

Still used in many situations, this style indents each new paragraph five spaces.

Dear Ms. Wright:

Thank you for your interest in Olley Manufacturing. At this time there are no openings, but with your qualifications, you'll soon find employment.
We'll keep your resume on record for one year. Please keep in touch with us, because when hiring begins, you'll be our first choice.

Left-margin Notation Paragraphs

This style gives one-word clues on the left margin as to the paragraph's content. Begin each paragraph with an engaging word and type it in capital letters. Indent the rest of the paragraph.

Dear Ms. Wright:

THANKS   for your interest in Olley Manufacturing. At this time there are no openings, but with your qualifications, you'll soon find employment.

RESUMES   are kept on record for one year. Please keep in touch with us, because when hiring begins, you'll be our first choice.

Numbered Paragraphs

This style is effective for long letters which include many topics or facts. It helps emphasize important points.

Dear Ms. Wright:

Thank you for your interest in Olley Manufacturing.

1. At this time there are no openings.
2. With your qualifications, you'll soon find employment.
3. We'll keep your resume on record for one year.

Please keep in touch with us, because when hiring begins, you'll be our first choice.

Unique Paragraphs

Imaginative paragraphs are eye-catching and often result-producing. However, visually effective paragraphs that seem *too* curious may arouse a lack of confidence from the more somber readers.

A rejection letter would NOT be an appropriate situation for this style. Unique paragraphs are best used in direct mailings or collection letters. Let your imagination be your guide.

This

Christmas

do something extra

special for your family!

Visit the Dawson Department Store

for ALL your personal shopping needs!

HO

HO

HO

Two final points to remember about paragraphs:

    1. Emphasis

        a. Placement

        b. Area

    2. Objectivity vs. Subjectivity

EMPHASIS

Emphasize words, ideas, and sentences by their placement.

WHERE you place words, ideas, and sentences is very important. Although the topic sentence is THE most significant part of any paragraph, positioning is also important. Your arrangement of words, ideas, and sentences helps the audience to focus on your exact meaning.

Place words correctly for emphasis.

Readers can misunderstand your meaning when words are misplaced. To accentuate your main idea, arrange your words properly. Reexamine your writing for confusing word order.

Notice the difference in emphasis, therefore in meaning, from the various locations of one word:

Only *I went to school.*	—	I'm the only one to go to school.
I **only** *went to school.*	—	I did nothing but go to school.
I went **only** *to school.*	—	I went nowhere else but to school.
I went to school **only**.	—	School was everything to me.

The following words are the most commonly misplaced:

about	almost	approximately	around
essentially	hardly	nearly	never
only	practically	roughly	virtually

To write clearly, place your words in the order that will stress your main points.

Place ideas correctly for emphasis.

Just as word placement shows emphasis, so does idea placement. Organize not only the words—but also the ideas WITHIN paragraphs—in classifications of time, space, and importance. Position ideas at one of two places:

1.   The **beginning** of a sentence
2.   The **end** of a sentence

For the greatest effectiveness, however, place the idea at the END of the sentence. WHY?

- ■   **The sentence builds momentum, builds to a climax**
- ■   **Since it's the last thing they read, the audience will remember it**

EXERCISE FOR IDEA EMPHASIS

Change this sentence to place the most important idea at its end:

To get the contract is the reason we should bid.

_____

Place sentences correctly for emphasis.

As you arrange words and ideas to stress your precise meaning, remember to arrange sentences correctly in each paragraph.

Begin with a topic sentence, followed by supporting sentences, a concluding sentence, and finally a transitional sentence.

Emphasize words, ideas, and sentences by the amount of area.

The amount of SPACE given to a detail emphasizes its importance.

If a large part of the paragraph describes one detail, the audience understands that this particular detail is important in relation to the rest of the paragraph.

OBJECTIVITY

Objective writing presents nothing but the FACTS. In most cases, objective writing is best. It relates the truth. It informs.

Objective writing is instructional. It describes or gives directions. Objective writing is used for HOW-TO manuals and descriptive or process reports.

Objective = Facts   **Subjective = Feelings**

2+2=4

SUBJECTIVITY

Subjective writing reveals your personal opinions. It shows your ATTITUDE toward the facts. It shows how you FEEL about them.

Read the following two paragraphs.

Which is informative and which is opinionated?

Which is objective and which is subjective?

1. It rained that day. She moved from her parents' home into her own apartment.

2. The overcast day reflected her mood. The rain only intensified her feelings of loneliness as she moved out of her parents' house. Fearfully she left the only home she had ever known and moved into her small, empty apartment.

> **OBJECTIVE is preferable when you want to present the facts. SUBJECTIVE is better if your purpose is to persuade. Subjective writing *slants* your writing to reflect your opinion.**

Persuasive Writing—AKA Subjective Writing

To write persuasively, first think of all the possible objections to your ideas. Next "answer" them by turning those negative objections into positive advantages. This will get attention and convince your readers to agree with your ideas.

By writing subjectively, you influence your readers.

Four steps to writing persuasively:

- List all possible objections
- Change objections into advantages
- Appeal to readers' imagination or foresight
- Convince readers to agree with your ideas

> **Be consistent. Never mix objective and subjective writing.**

EXERCISE FOR OBJECTIVE WRITING

Write an objective paragraph about the following topic. Imagine that it is for a GEOLOGY TEXTBOOK. Do not allow any opinion or attitude to influence your writing. Present only the facts. Describe the educational features.

TOPIC: A snowcapped mountain in the morning

_____

_____

_____

_____

_____

_____

_____

===

EXERCISE FOR SUBJECTIVE WRITING

Write a subjective paragraph about the following topic. Imagine that it is for a
TRAVEL BROCHURE. Color your writing with your personal opinion or attitude.
Influence your readers. Persuade your readers to visit this beautiful area.

TOPIC: A snowcapped mountain in the morning

_____

_____

_____

_____

_____

_____

===

MEETINGS, AGENDAS, AND MINUTES

A formal meeting requires an agenda. An agenda is a listing of the meeting's time, place, and items of business for discussion. The writing of the agenda is the responsibility of the committee's Secretary.

SAMPLE AGENDA

AGENDA

FOR THE MEETING OF THE

OPERATIONS COMMITTEE

TO BE HELD IN ROOM H 209

AT 2:00 P.M.

ON JUNE 24, 19--

1. Reading and endorsement of Minutes of Operations Committee Meeting held at 2:00 P.M. on May 23, 19--.

2. Matters originating from Minutes.

3. To consider new building site for satellite office.

4. To appraise new manual of operations.

5. To estimate costs of expansion.

6. To entertain discussion of other New Business.

7. Determine place, time, and date of next meeting.

Reading the Agenda:

The heading indicates the place, time, and date of the committee meeting.

1. The Minutes from the previous meeting are approved or corrected by committee members. The reading of the Minutes can be accomplished in one of two ways:

     a. Minutes distributed and read before meeting.
     b. Minutes read aloud at meeting.

2. Now follows a discussion of matters originating from the Minutes. This is the time to take care of "Old Business."

3. "New Business" is discussed. All new items of Business are introduced through an infinitive verb **(TO....)**:

     a. To consider....
     b. To discuss....
     c. To entertain....

4. "New Business" is discussed.

5. "New Business" is discussed.

6. Any other items of "New Business" are discussed.

7. The place, time, and date of the next meeting are decided.

MINUTES FORMAT

Taking notes at meetings and then transferring them into Minutes requires a special form. Minutes are a summary of what happened at the meeting. In effect, Minutes are short reports. Not every single word is recorded. Instead, a synopsis is written that indicates the results of the meeting.

Remember these three elements when writing Minutes:

     1.   The tone is formal

     2.   The verbs are passive

     3.   The vocabulary is conventional

For more information regarding tone, see the **REPORTS' TONE: LEVELS OF FORMALITY** section. **CHAPTER 17**

For more information regarding passive verbs, see the **LIGHTS, CAMERAS, VERBS!** segment of the **PARTS AND PARCELS OF SPEECH** section. **CHAPTER 9**

Vocabulary

Following are the proper word choices for varying situations:

- If the committee listened to a report/suggestion, write:

  The committee...

heard	
noted	*(that)*
recognized	
recorded	

  <u>*The committee heard the report*</u>.

- If the committee thought it best to take some action, write:

  The committee...

agreed	*(to)*
conceded	*(that)*
concurred	
decided	
found	
resolved	

  <u>*The committee resolved to purchase the warehouse*</u>.

- If the committee thought it best not to take some action, write:

  The committee...

declined	
agreed not	*(to)*
refused	
rejected	

  <u>*The committee rejected the proposal to purchase the warehouse*</u>.

- If the committee received instructions, write:

  The committee was...

advised	*(that)*
informed	
instructed	*(to)*
notified	

  <u>*The committee was notified of the guidelines*</u>.

- If the committee decided to wait, write:

  The committee...

  > *deferred*
  > *postponed*
  > *shelved*
  > *tabled*

  <u>*The committee shelved the proposal.*</u>

Because Minutes are a special kind of business writing, they require a certain format. Except for several additions, they follow the same pattern as that of the Agenda.

- Heading
- Attendants
- Nonattendants
- Special attendants
- Endorsement of Minutes
- Items of old and new business
- Place, time, and date of next meeting
- Signatures of Chairperson and Secretary

The heading reads as follows:

MINUTES

FOR THE MEETING OF THE

OPERATIONS COMMITTEE

HELD IN ROOM H 209

AT 2:00 P.M.

ON JUNE 24, 19--

The Agenda's verb is not used in the future tense. The verb is the past tense "HELD," not "TO BE HELD."

The attending committee members and their titles are listed.

The following members were in attendance:
(**OR** Present:)

Sara Simms, Chairperson
Howard Lin, Director of Operations
Jim Dawes, Director of Personnel
Joyce Liu, Vice President of International Relations
James Chou, Treasurer

The committee members who did not attend are also listed:

The following members were not in attendance:
(**OR** Not Present:)
(**OR** Apologies for Absence:)

Ken Smith, Supervisor of Operations

People who attended the meeting by invitation are listed:

Present by Invitation:
(**OR** Present by Invitation for Item Three:)

Members' endorsement or correction of Minutes is indicated.

The business discussions are recorded in the same order and number as were listed on the meeting's agenda.

To consider new building site for satellite office.

After consultation, it was decided that the site was unacceptable because of zoning restrictions.

To appraise new manual of operations.

After deliberation, the committee resolved to appoint a subcommittee to further review the manual.

The subcommittee membership includes the following people:

Howard Lin, Director of Operations
Jim Dawes, Director of Personnel
Joyce Liu, Vice President of International Relations

Report the place, time, and date of the following meeting.

At the conclusion of the Minutes, two lines are typed for the signatures of the Chairperson and the Secretary of the committee.

The Secretary signs and dates the Minutes as soon as they are written. If all data is correct, the Chairperson will sign and date the Minutes within two days after the committee meeting.

Determine place, time, and date of next meeting.

It was concurred that the subsequent meeting of the committee will be held at 3:00 P.M. on August 1, 19-- in room H 209.

_____
Chairperson
June 26, 19--

_____
Secretary
June 24, 19--

BUSINESS CORRESPONDENCE

13

OR LETTER WRITING

Just as with fictional writing and report writing, letter writing demands three things: a beginning, a middle, and an ending. However, before you begin the actual process of writing, think:

Plan

WHAT YOU WANT TO SAY AND

HOW YOU WANT TO SAY IT.

WHY are you writing this letter? To calm an angry customer? To write a purchase order? To bid on a contract? *Think!!*

First YOU have to clearly understand your reason for writing, so that the READERS will clearly understand you.

- First know WHY you're writing.
- Next decide WHAT to write.

LETTER STRUCTURE AND CONTENT

The easiest way to write a letter is to work from a blueprint. Use these guidelines to organize your main topics in letter writing. Photocopy blank pages of the following blueprint so that you can arrange your thoughts for each letter before you actually write it.

EXERCISE FOR BUSINESS CORRESPONDENCE

---

1. Fill in the blanks of each question
2. Circle which tactic(s) best suit each letter
3. Circle which tone(s) best suit each letter
4. Then write the letter

Correspondence Blueprint

Is purpose to answer or initiate letter? Why?

_____

What is appropriate thank you or pleasantry?

_____

What information or action is needed by correspondent?

_____

Can information be given or action be performed? Why?

_____

How can correspondent benefit?

_____

How can I or my company benefit?

_____

What issues should I address?

_____

What tactic(s) should I use? (circle)

Apology	*I'm / We're sorry*
Appreciation	*Thank you*
Clarification	*Please allow me/us to explain*
Complaint	*Unfortunately, the check was not*
Compliment	*Your references are sensational!*
Concession	*I / We will be most happy to*
Concern	*It has come to my/our attention that*
Congratulations	*I / We applaud you for your*
Cooperation	*Would you be willing*
Curiosity arousal	*Retire in three years!*
Diplomatic	*I / We empathize with your situation*
Gratitude	*I / We are indebted to you*
Information gathering	*Could you please supply the data*
Information giving	*I / We would be pleased to assist*
Positive	*It is my/our pleasure to inform you*
Urgency	*I / We understand how anxious you must*

What tone should I take? (circle)

Formal   Humorous   Personal   Stern   Understanding

CORRESPONDENCE BLUEPRINTS make letter writing easy. Because they help you sort out your ideas, concerns, issues, goals, and needs, they do the work for you. The key to effective letter writing is organization.

CORRESPONDENCE BLUEPRINTS help in these ways:

- Organize thoughts
- Compose letters that are easy to understand
- Address all issues, all points
- Answer all questions, all concerns
- Generate letters that are shorter, more concise

In addition to these advantages, designing what you are going to write has another benefit:

TONE

It allows you to choose the best TONE for your purpose. Do you want to be polite, demanding, stern? As always, remember your readers. Write in the tone best suited for THEM and for YOU.

For more information on tone and word choice, see the **REPORTS' TONE: LEVELS OF FORMALITY** section. **CHAPTER 17**

Let's try putting this CORRESPONDENCE BLUEPRINT method into practice with a sample letter received from an angry customer:

To Whom It May Concern:

For sixteen years I have been a premium-paying customer of Purple Cross Health Insurance.

Last month my daughter broke her wrist, and I placed my first claim with your company—after SIXTEEN YEARS!

To date, neither I nor my doctor has received payment, but the doctor demands to be paid, or he says my credit rating will be threatened. I am furious!

Please remit payment immediately! Also cancel my policy!

Doug Jones
Policy # 000000000

Is this client angry? YES!!! Tact and good customer relations are called for. These require calming your clients and giving them the finest service possible. The best way to handle these is to compose your thoughts before you compose your letter. Use the CORRESPONDENCE BLUEPRINT to shape your main purposes and points.

Correspondence Blueprint

IS PURPOSE TO ANSWER OR INITIATE LETTER? WHY?

- To answer Mr. Jones
- To placate his anger
- To pay his claim, if possible
- To make him a satisfied customer

WHAT IS APPROPRIATE THANK YOU OR PLEASANTRY?

Thank you for bringing this matter to our attention.

We appreciate conscientious customers, such as yourself.

We apologize for any inconvenience to you.

WHAT INFORMATION OR ACTION IS NEEDED BY CORRESPONDENT?

- Needs reason(s) why claim has not been paid
- Needs reassurance that our company will provide it, if possible
- Needs to know we understand his concern
- Needs payment made as soon as possible
- Needs communication to doctor (provider)

CAN INFORMATION BE GIVEN OR ACTION BE PERFORMED? WHY?

- Yes, his policy does cover such benefits.
- We are pleased to inform him of it.
- Report that claim has not been received by provider.
- Report that we will request claim from provider.
- Reassure that upon receipt, claim WILL be processed.
- Turnaround time is two weeks.

HOW CAN CORRESPONDENT BENEFIT?

- Relief from knowledge that claim will be paid
- Relief from knowledge that his credit rating will remain intact
- Confirmation of honesty of our company

HOW CAN I OR MY COMPANY BENEFIT?

- A satisfied customer
- Good word-of-mouth advertising for company
- My interpersonal skills will be noticed by manager

WHAT ISSUES SHOULD I ADDRESS?

- Customer's satisfaction
- Provider's (doctor's) cooperation IF s/he wants prompt payment
- Proof of company's honesty

WHAT TONE SHOULD I TAKE?

Formal   Humorous   Personal   Stern   Understanding

All right, now you know what TACTICS and TONE to use. You know what ISSUES to address, what QUESTIONS to answer. You know what ACTION is needed and how the consumer (and you) can BENEFIT.

THE WORK IS DONE.

All that's left is writing the letter:

CUSTOMER'S EXPLANATION

PURPLE CROSS INSURANCE UNITED
9 South Bend Avenue
Bangkok, Thailand

Telephone: (000) 000-0000

June 20, 19--

Dear Mr. Jones:
        Thank you for bringing this matter to our attention.
Purple Cross values conscientious customers, such as yourself,
and we apologize for any inconvenience to you.
        We are pleased to confirm that your policy does cover
such benefits as your daughter's accident. Purple Cross will be
happy to honor your claim as soon as it is received from your
doctor or provider.
        Apparently your provider neglected to forward the
necessary paperwork. We have already requested the claim
from your provider. Because it is your physician's obligation
to submit the claim, let us assure you that you are under no
threat of a lowered credit rating.
        As soon as we receive it, your claim will be processed.
Our turnaround time is two weeks. To further put your mind at
ease, we will keep you updated as to the progress of your claim.
When it is received from your physician, we will photocopy it and
forward it to you.
        Again, we sincerely apologize for any inconvenience,
and we do hope you will reconsider and remain one of Purple
Cross's three million satisfied customers.

Very truly yours,

Bill Blah
Customer Service Department

LETTER LAYOUT OR FORMAT

In letter writing, one BIG rule differs from report writing:

- FIRST address your <u>most</u> important point
- NEXT address your <u>less</u> important points

Formula for Letters

1st paragraph	—	Introduction
2nd paragraph	—	**Most** important point
3rd paragraph	—	**Second** most important point
4th paragraph	—	**Least** important point
5th paragraph	—	Conclusion
	—	Call to Action

Like paragraphs, memos, and reports, letters have three things:

Beginning	—	Introduction
Middle	—	Body of Material or Content
End	—	Conclusion
	—	Call to Action

BEGINNING

The **first** paragraph introduces you and your subject.

First impressions are the most lasting, so open your letter with an interesting, appropriate bit of information.

If at all possible, thank the readers for something. Thank them for their interest, their understanding, their patience, their concern, but try to start each letter with a note of appreciation.

Then use one or more of the following tactics:

- Be **positive** — stress the positive aspects
  - downplay the negative aspects
- Be **tactful** — show respect
- Be **direct** — get to the point quickly
- Be **polite** — downplay their errors
- Be **selfless** — use **YOU**, not I/me/my/we/our

- Be **interesting** — pique their curiosity
- Be **inquisitive** — ask direct questions
    - ask rhetorical questions: (e.g., What is efficiency?)
- Be **honest**   — admit any mistake or error
- Be **humble**   — ask for help, advice, teamwork
- Be **kind**   — be understanding or sympathetic
- Be **helpful**   — identify yourself
    - identify your company
    - identify your reason for writing

MIDDLE

The **next** paragraphs contain the important issue(s).

Just as the beginning of a letter is the introductory portion, the middle of the letter is the main part which contains the reasons why you are writing.

In the middle of the letter, explain all of the issue's aspects:

- HOW
- WHAT
- WHEN
- WHERE
- WHO
- WHY

LETTER TONE AND STYLE

Remember the five C's of letter writing:

1.	**Clearness**	—	avoid jargon
2.	**Completeness**	—	include all facts
3.	**Conciseness**	—	choose the right word
4.	**Correctness**	—	proofread and edit
5.	**Courteousness**	—	be polite

Clearness

Thinking that it increases the professional tone of their writing, many business people use needlessly large words. This "language" of the business world is called jargon. For clear writing, AVOID jargon. Use simple, direct language.

> For more information, see the **BUSINESS-ESE OR BUSINESS JARGON** segment of the **WORDS AND HOW THEY WORK** section. **CHAPTER 8**

Completeness

Include all necessary information WITHIN the letter. Assume that the readers do not know all the facts. Make it easy for the readers to understand your situation. Spell it out for them.

Conciseness

As with all forms of writing, be specific. Say what you mean CLEARLY. Don't be vague or confusing.

BE SPECIFIC:

BE	DON'T BE
Concrete	Abstract
Clear	Confusing
Objective	Subjective
Active	Passive
Specific	General

> For more information, see the **NOUNS OR WHAT'S IN A NAME?** segment of the **PARTS AND PARCELS OF SPEECH** section. **CHAPTER 9**

Correctness

Always proofread and edit your letters.

> For more information, refer to the **EDITING, REWRITING, AND POLISHING** section. **CHAPTER 19**

Courteousness

Use common courtesy—which seems to be uncommon these days.

Use the proper salutations:

> **Formal** —*Dear Mr. Jones:*
>
> **Informal**—*Dear John,*

Avoid phrases that scold or annoy:

> *As we mentioned previously*
>
> *As you are aware*
>
> *If you had paid attention*
>
> *Obviously, you should have*
>
> *You are mistaken*
>
> *You are wrong*

Use updated letter endings that are polite without being old-fashioned, yet still end on a friendly note:

> *We appreciate your cooperation.*
>
> *Thanks again for your interest.*
>
> *Your order will be mailed the moment it's done.*
>
> **NOT** —*Anticipating your answer, I am,*
>
> **NOT** —*Expecting to hear from you, I remain,*

Use the correct closings:

> *Sincerely,*
>
> *Sincerely yours,*
>
> *Yours truly,*
>
> *Very truly yours,*

ENDING—CONCLUSION

Conclude your letter with a summary or a restatement of purpose, then follow with a call to action.

A letter's ending is like a movie's climax. It's the most important part. Why? Because it's the reader's <u>last</u> impression. It's what the reader remembers.

Depending upon the reason for writing the letter, use one of these endings:

Be **appreciative**	—	*Thank you for remembering us. We're eager to repay the favor.*
Be **assuring**	—	*Unfortunately your policy does not cover this. However, we'll make every effort to see that you get all available benefits!*
Be **firm but tactful**	—	*We're sorry, but we're not able to make an exception.*
Be **inquisitive**	—	*How much capital are you willing to invest in our venture?*
Be **polite**	—	*We're always pleased to explain our service policies!*
Be **pragmatic**	—	*Thanks but no thanks right now. However, things may change.*
Be **selfless**	—	Use **YOU**, not I/me/my/we/our
Be **sorry**	—	*We sincerely apologize for the delay. Thanks for your patience.*
Be **time-conscious**	—	*We look forward to the meeting Monday at 10 A.M.!*

ENDINGS

Call to Action

Make your endings STRONG. Weak endings accomplish nothing. Strong endings cause prompt action. **Specifically** tell your readers:

- WHAT you want
- WHEN you want it
- HOW you want it done

Don't expect your readers to be self-starters. Don't expect them to jump into motion by themselves. They're human; they want to delay things until the last possible moment. They need impetus.

Motivating Closes

YOU MUST PUSH YOUR READERS INTO ACTION

How do you push your readers? Give them strong endings!

Try these result-producing endings:

Fax us the necessary paperwork by Tuesday, July 19,
so we can draw up the contract. Dial (000) 000-0000.

The deadline for bidding is 1:00 P.M., Friday, May 2.
Submit your bid today in the enclosed, self-addressed envelope.

These endings tell your readers **four** important points:

1.   WHAT you want
2.   WHEN you want it
3.   HOW you want it done

   and

4.   **WHY it's easy**

Make it easy for your readers. Make it SOUND easy. Emphasize how simple it is to act NOW.

Try more of these motivators:

Our fax machine operates 24 hours a day. Fax us NOW
at 000-000-0000.

Dial our toll-free number any time night or day!
(800) 000-0000 Just do it NOW!

Call our office collect the MOMENT you have the
results! (000) 000-0000

Enclosed is a self-addressed, stamped envelope (SASE).
Drop this order in the mail today!

Enclosed is a self-addressed postcard. Initial it and mail it.
Your order will be shipped the same day we receive the card.

These action-prompters are positive in their approach:

DO THIS! IT'S EASY!

There's another way to enlist your readers' cooperation:
Use reverse psychology. Don't make it easy to say **yes**; make it
difficult to say **no**!

IT'S EASY! DON'T DO ANYTHING!

Unless we hear differently, your order will be
shipped the first of the month.

Your tape/album/CD/book will automatically be
sent to your mailing address. Should you NOT
wish the selection-of-the-month sent, check the
appropriate box and postmark it no later than
April 15th.

Order today! If not completely satisfied,
tell us why and return it for a full refund.

MECHANICS OF LETTERS

The basics of correspondence require certain forms.
There are five key types of correspondence:

1. Private Person to Private Person (or Friend to Friend)
2. Private Person to Business
3. Person to Person WITHIN Business (or Memo)
4. Business to Private Person
5. Business to Business

Private Person to Private Person

The style and tone for the first type, Friend to Friend, are informal, as reflected in the casual structure of the following letter:

29 Fifth Street
New York, New York 10001
(000) 000-0000
June 20, 19--

Dear Harry,

Thanks again....

Sincerely,

FIVE ELEMENTS TO A PERSONAL LETTER

LETTER 1

Personal Letter

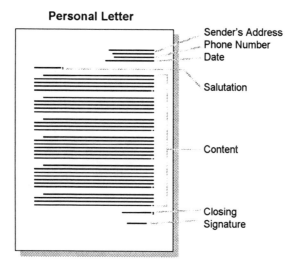

A friendly letter consists of <u>FIVE</u> elements:

1. Heading

    Address

    Phone Number

    Date

2. Salutation

3. Content

4. Closing

5. Signature

Heading: The only appearing address is that of the sender.

Placement is in upper right-hand corner.

The sender's phone number appears under address.

Date letter is written appears under address.

Salutation: First name basis, followed by a comma—NOT a colon.

Content: Friendly, informal tone and language.

Paragraphs are often indented five spaces.

Closing:	Familiar, even intimate wording, followed by comma. Sincerely yours and Love are also correct. Placement is to the right of the middle of the page.
Signature:	First or given name need only be signed. Placement is centered under Closing.

Private Person to Business

The style and tone for the Private Person to Business are more formal than for that of Friends:

---

22 Briarwood Drive

Chicago, IL 60600

(000) 000-0000

December 24, 19--

Mr. John Marden

Marden Sporting Goods

77 Sunset Strip

Los Angeles, CA 00000

Dear Mr. Marden:

In regard to item #334 in the Christmas catalogue....

Yours truly,

Justine Evans

SIX ELEMENTS TO A BUSINESS LETTER

LETTER 2

Private Person to Business Letter

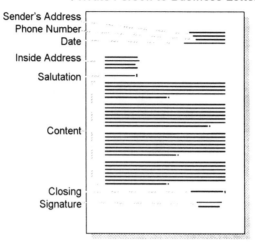

A business letter contains <u>SIX</u> elements:

1. Heading
2. Inside Address
3. Salutation
4. Content
5. Closing
6. Signature

Heading: Consists of Person's address, phone number, and date. Placement is in upper right-hand corner.

Inside Address: Consists of name of Person and Business to whom Person is writing and address of Business. Placement is on left margin, four typewriter spaces below Heading.

Salutation: Greeting is formal and appears on left margin, two typewriter spaces below the inside address.

Dear Mr./Ms./Mrs./Miss Stevens is correct if name
is known. If name is not known, Dear Sir(s)/Dear
Madam/Dear Mesdames (feminine plural) is fine.
This is always followed by a colon—NOT a comma.

Content: First line of content is on left margin, two
typewriter spaces below Salutation.
If block-style is not used, indent each paragraph
five spaces from left margin.

Closing: Business standard closings such as, Yours truly
or Very truly yours are preferred. Appears to
the right of middle and is followed by comma.

Signature: Two signatures appear: one handwritten above
one typewritten. Placement is beneath Closing.

Memo

The style and tone for the Person to Person WITHIN Business Letter (or
Memo) follow those for memos and short reports.

LETTER 3

Memo

TO:
FROM:
DATE:
RE:

Subject Heading

Content

For more information, refer to the **IN-HOUSE MEMOS AND SHORT
REPORTS** section. **CHAPTER 15**

Business to Private Person

The style and tone for the Business to Private Person Letter are quite formal. The letter contains the six elements of business correspondence:

1. Heading
2. Inside Address
3. Salutation
4. Content
5. Closing
6. Signature

DAWSON, WEST, AND WELLS, INC.

16 Washington Square

Chetek, Oregon 00000

PHONE: (000) 000-0000   FAX: (000) 000-0000

July 5, 19--

Ms. Chen

3F, #4, Lane 5, Nanking W. Rd.

Taipei, Taiwan ROC

Dear Ms. Chen:

Your payment was received....

Very truly yours,

Clem Samuels

President

LETTER 4

Business to Private Person Letter

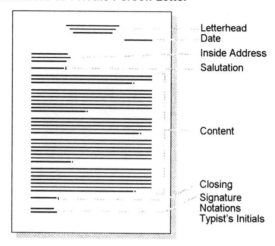

	Letterhead
	Date
	Inside Address
	Salutation
	Content
	Closing
	Signature
	Notations
	Typist's Initials

Heading: Stationery containing a letterhead needs only the
                      date added. If Business has no stationery with a
                      letterhead, then heading will consist of Business's
                      address, phone number, fax or Telex number, and
                      date. Placement is in upper right-hand corner.

Inside Address: Consists of name and address of Person to whom letter
                      is written. Placement is on left margin, four typewriter
                      spaces below Heading.

Salutation: Greeting is formal and appears on left margin, two
                      typewriter spaces below the inside address.
                      Dear Mr./Ms./Mrs./Miss Stevens is correct if name is
                      known. If name is not known, Dear Sir(s)/Dear
                      Madam/Dear Mesdames (feminine plural) is fine. This is
                      always followed by a colon—NOT a comma.

. Content: First line of content is on left margin, two spaces below
                      Salutation. If block-style is not used, indent each
                      paragraph five spaces from left margin.

Closing: Business standard closings such as, Yours truly or Very
                      truly yours are preferred. Appears at left margin and is
                      followed by comma.

Signature: Two signatures appear: one handwritten above one
                      typewritten. Placement is beneath Closing. If desired,
                      writer's title may appear under that.

Business to Business

The style and tone for the Business to Business Letter are the most formal. The letter contains the six elements of business correspondence:

1. Heading
2. Inside Address
3. Salutation
4. Content
5. Closing
6. Signature

DAWSON, WEST, AND WELLS, INC.

16 Washington Square

Chetek, Oregon 00000

PHONE: (000) 000-0000   FAX: (000) 000-0000

July 5, 19--

Mr. Howard Liu

Vice President

National Bank of Taiwan

Nanking East Road

Taipei, Taiwan ROC

Dear Mr. Liu:

In consideration of the account....

Yours truly,

Clem Samuels

Encl.

c.c. Ms. Grace Chen

CF/kb

LETTER 5

Business to Business Letter

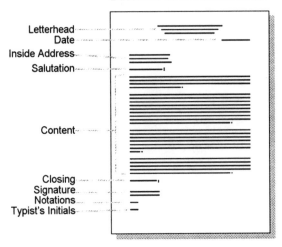

Letterhead
Date
Inside Address
Salutation

Content

Closing
Signature
Notations
Typist's Initials

Heading:	Stationery containing a letterhead needs only the date added. If Business has no stationery with a letterhead, then heading will consist of Business's address, phone number, fax or Telex number, and date. Placement is in upper right-hand corner.
Inside Address:	Consists of name and address of Contact Person and Business to whom letter is written. Placement is on left margin, four typewriter spaces below Heading.
Salutation:	Greeting is formal and appears on left margin, two typewriter spaces below the inside address. <u>Dear Mr./Ms./Mrs./Miss</u> Stevens is correct if name is known. If name is not known, <u>Dear Sir(s)/Dear Madam/Dear Mesdames (feminine plural)</u> is fine. This is always followed by a colon—NOT a comma.
Content:	First line of content is on left margin, two typewriter spaces below Salutation. If block-style is not used, indent each paragraph five spaces from left margin.
Closing:	Business standard closings such as, <u>Yours truly</u> or <u>Very truly yours</u> are preferred. Appears at left margin and is followed by comma.

Signature:	Two signatures appear: one handwritten above one typewritten. Placement is beneath Closing. If desired, writer's title may appear under that.
Encl.:	Enclosures. This refers to any additional information, charts, graphics, or data that is enclosed with the letter.
c.c.:	Carbon copy. Although very few copies of letters are made with carbon paper any more, the c.c. means that a photocopy or a duplicate of the letter has been sent to the person indicated.
CF/kb:	The capitalized letters are the initials of the letter's author. The small letters are the initials of the letter's typist.

ENVELOPES

After writing the letter, you must address an envelope in the same style and tone as those of the letter.

Sender's Address

In all cases, the name and address of the sender should appear in the upper left-hand corner of the front of the envelope or in the upper center of the envelope's back.

Recipient's Address

The address appears slightly left of the envelope's center. The address of the envelope should be exactly the same as that of the letter.

If mailing internationally, be sure to include the name of the country.

Private Person to Private Person (or Friend to Friend)

James Smith
29 Fifth Street
New York, New York 10001

        Mr. Harry Baughman
        18 North Lane
        Summit, IL 60600

Private Person to Business

Justine Evans
22 Briarwood Drive
Chicago, IL 60600

        Mr. John Marden
        Marden Sporting Goods
        77 Sunset Strip
        Los Angeles, CA 00000

Person to Person within Business (or Memo)

Within the same building, memos are usually hand delivered.

If mailed to another office, follow the same procedure as for a Business to Business envelope.

For more information, refer to the **IN-HOUSE MEMOS AND SHORT REPORTS** section. **CHAPTER 15**

Business to Private Person

```
Dawson, West, and Wells, Inc.
16 Washington Square
Chetek, Oregon 00000
USA
                    Ms. Chen
                    3F, #4, Lane 5, Nanking W. Rd.
                    Taipei, Taiwan ROC
```

Business to Business

Notice that the recipient, the recipient's title, the company's name, and address are all clearly expressed.

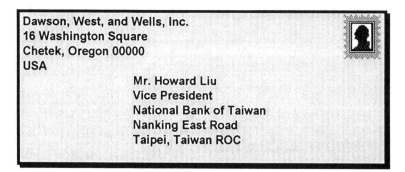

```
Dawson, West, and Wells, Inc.
16 Washington Square
Chetek, Oregon 00000
USA
                    Mr. Howard Liu
                    Vice President
                    National Bank of Taiwan
                    Nanking East Road
                    Taipei, Taiwan ROC
```

An alternate form of addressing a Business to Business letter is as follows. Note that only the company's name and address appear slightly left of the envelope's center. The recipient's name and title appear on the far left of the envelope, beneath the word **Attention**, which is followed by a colon.

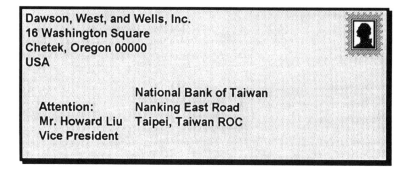

```
Dawson, West, and Wells, Inc.
16 Washington Square
Chetek, Oregon 00000
USA

                    National Bank of Taiwan
Attention:          Nanking East Road
Mr. Howard Liu      Taipei, Taiwan ROC
Vice President
```

CATEGORIES OF BUSINESS LETTERS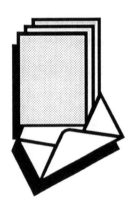

14

Just as there are various styles of writing for reports, there are different kinds of letter writing for diverse occasions. This section includes three basic categories of business letters and their answers, both granting (saying YES), and refusing (saying NO).

1. Letters of Query, Request
   - Letters Granting Requests
   - Letters Refusing Requests
2. Letters of Complaint, Claim, and Adjustment
   - Letters Granting Claims
   - Letters Refusing Claims
3. Sales Letters or Direct Mailings

LETTERS OF QUERY, REQUEST

Queries are questions. There are two types of queries:

1. **Solicited** Letters of Query   Writers answer advertisement and request more information about that company or order its product(s).

2. **Unsolicited** Letters of Query   Writers begin correspondence and request more information about a company or ordering a product.

Most often it's a Private Person who writes a query to a Business. However, letters of query are also written from one Person to another Person within a Business (a Memo), a Business to a Private Person, or a Business to another Business.

No matter which type of correspondence, the most important element of a query letter is clarity:

Write Clearly!

Solicited Query

Example of Solicited Query:

---

22 Briarwood Drive
Chicago, IL 60600
(000) 000-0000
December 4, 19--

Marden Sporting Goods
77 Sunset Strip
Los Angeles, CA 00000

Gentlemen:

In regard to your advertisement in <u>The Daily News</u>, please send me a copy of your Christmas catalogue.

Yours truly,

Justine Evans

Remember four things when writing a solicited query letter:

1. Be clear—state EXACTLY what you want
2. Be brief—get to the point
3. Include your address and phone number!!!
4. Mention where you saw the advertisement

Unsolicited Query

An unsolicited query letter is a bit more complicated. It often asks for detailed answers to complex questions. Your job is to make the letter as simple as possible for the reader to answer.

KIS
KEEP IT SIMPLE.

When asking readers questions, remember that you are really asking for their time. Be considerate. Be brief.

IF YOU WANT ANSWERS—MAKE YOUR QUESTIONS EASY TO UNDERSTAND.

1. Be specific—quickly state the following:

- WHAT you want
- WHY you want it
- WHEN you want it
- WHO you are

2. List questions

- Use numbers to identify each question [1) 2) 3)]
- Indent each question five spaces from left margin

3. Thank readers for their time

IF YOU WANT RESPONSES—MAKE YOUR QUESTIONS EVEN EASIER TO ANSWER.

1. Phrase questions for easy answering

- Ask YES OR NO questions that can be checked ✓ or circled O

    Can YZ company supply 100 gross by 7/1/96?

    ☑ *Yes*

    ☐ *No*

- Ask questions needing **ONE or TWO WORD** answers

  *How many cars are needed?*_____ _____

  *Manual shift or automatic?*_____ _____

- Provide MULTIPLE CHOICE answers that can be checked ✓ or circled O

  What color shirts do you have?

  Red

  White

  Blue

2. Mail queries during slow business times

  DO NOT mail during Lunar New Year

  DO NOT mail during Christmas

3. Describe how READERS will benefit by answering

4. Include SASE (Self-Addressed Stamped Envelope)

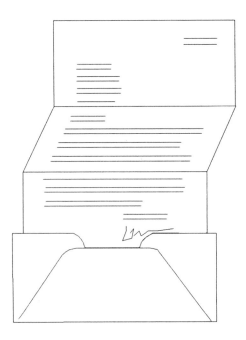

UNSOLICITED QUERY

DAWSON, WEST, AND WELLS, INC.
16 Washington Square
Chetek, Oregon 00000
PHONE: (000) 000-0000   FAX: (000) 000-0000

                                              July 5, 19--

Ms. Chen
3F, #4, Lane 5, Nanking W. Rd.
Taipei, Taiwan ROC

Dear Ms. Chen:

As one of our subscribers to World of Trust Funds Magazine,
YOUR opinion is vital in helping us to provide information that
YOU need for YOUR portfolio.

Would YOU take five minutes from YOUR busy schedule to fill
out this form? Our goal is to give YOU up-to-the-minute
information that will help YOU to meet YOUR financial goals.

YOUR net yearly income is:
Under $50,000
$50,000 → $100,000
$100,001 → $200,000
Over $200,000

Page 1

YOUR total assets are:
Under $50,000
$50,000 → $100,000
$100,001 → $200,000
Over $200,000

YOUR chief investment is:
Stocks
Bonds
Real Estate

Thank YOU for YOUR time! We understand that time is money,
so a SASE is enclosed for YOUR convenience.

Very truly YOURS,

Clem Samuels
President

Page 2

ANSWERS TO QUERIES, REQUESTS

Remember, when your company receives a query requesting more
information, it is really a purchase order in disguise.

Treat these writers as customers, and they will become customers. Be
aware of the tone and content of your letter.

Keep these things in mind when answering queries:

- Be polite; "Honey catches more flies than vinegar."
  Courtesy catches more customers than rudeness.

- Be prompt; don't keep writer waiting for your answer.

- Be helpful; answer each question clearly.

- Be interested; spell name and address correctly.

- Be specific; refer to enclosed information or catalog.

The basic answer to all questions is either YES or NO.
This can be phrased another way: granting or refusing a request.

- YES—Granting a Request
- NO—Refusing a Request

YES — Granting a Request

Saying YES to a prospective customer is a great opportunity to create good will and future sales.

Keep these things in mind when granting a request for information:

- Mention the enclosed material, catalogue or brochure.
- Answer each question in detail.
- State how you will follow up this letter.
- Keep the tone personal and friendly.

Dear Ms. Simms:

Thank you for requesting our brochure, "How to Increase Workplace Efficiency." We have included that brochure and another, "How to Upgrade Your Filing System."

Correct partitioning placement is critical to your traffic flow and efficiency. To answer your question regarding office expansion, please note the diagrams on page 15 of "How to Increase Workplace Efficiency." Three examples of pedestrian traffic and partitioning are shown; the third example takes into account your need for a larger filing area.

The second brochure, "How to Upgrade Your Filing System," provides helpful hints on more effective use of current filing space, while allowing for expansion.

We hope these brochures will be of service. Our architect, Mr. Smythe, will make an appointment with you next week to answer any further questions you may have about your office expansion. Thank you for the opportunity of assisting you with your plans.

Yours truly,

Saying YES to a request is not only enjoyable, but profitable.

Time spent answering questions is time spent gaining new clients.

Your answers can turn Queries into Purchase Orders.

TURN QUERIES INTO PURCHASE ORDERS

When answering queries or requests, just remember these things:

- Be prompt
- Be helpful, specific
- Be polite
- Be friendly
- Be available for further assistance (but NOT pushy)

NO — *Refusing a Request*

Saying NO to a request is a bit more difficult. The tone is important.

Remember these things when refusing a request:

- Thank the writer.
- Be direct and firm in your refusal.
- Be helpful—offer suggestions, explanations.
- Offer your services in the future.

Dear Mr. Simms:

Thank you for your interest in our employee, Mr. Brandon, in regard to his membership in social organizations.

We regret that we cannot release personal information about our employees because it would infringe upon their rights. However, we can do two things. First, we would like to recommend Mr. Brandon's fine character. Second, if you like, we will forward your inquiry to Mr. Brandon for him to answer himself.

Please do not hesitate to contact us if we can be of assistance in the future. Best wishes in your endeavors.

Yours truly,

When refusing a request, your tone is very important. Keep these tips in mind when writing a letter that refuses a request:

- Be **Diplomatic**   Do **NOT** make enemies
- Be **Prompt**   Do **NOT** delay
- Be **Polite**   Do **NOT** offend
- Be **Firm**   Do **NOT** give in
- SOMETIMES Be **Impersonal**   **CONSIDER** using passive voice

For more information, refer to the **ACTIVE AND PASSIVE VOICE** segment of the **LIGHTS, CAMERAS, VERBS!** section. **CHAPTER 9**

LETTERS OF COMPLAINT, CLAIM, AND ADJUSTMENT

A *letter of complaint* is an objection, a criticism of something.

A *claim letter* is a demand for action. Often the two are combined.

As an example, if you purchase a copier that constantly needs repair, you might write a letter to the copy machine company that **complains** about the situation and **demands** prompt action. This letter would be both a complaint and claim.

ADVICE: COUNT TO *TEN*

When writing either a complaint or claim letter, the best advice is to count to ten. In other words, THINK before you write. Don't write when you are angry; give yourself time to calm down and be reasonable. Again, your tone is all important:

1. Use facts, not feelings with letters of complaint or claim.

2. Try to remain as emotionally removed as possible.

3. Be professional.

4. Emphasize your willingness to cooperate.

5. Emphasize desire for mutual satisfaction for you and reader.

How to Write a Letter of Complaint or Claim

After elimination of your anger at the situation or the persons responsible for it, compose a letter with these points in mind:

1. Describe the problem SPECIFICALLY
    - State date of purchase
    - State purchase and/or repair costs
    - State make, model, or serial numbers
    - State color, style, size
    - State any other pertinent information

2. Describe the resulting trouble or damage

3. Appeal to reader's obligations
    - Moral obligation, sense of decency
    - Business obligation, sense of duty
    - Future goodwill in business relationship

4. ONLY THREATEN WHEN REPEATED ATTEMPTS FAIL
    - Threaten loss of business
    - Threaten legal action

5. Recommend action
    - State action you consider fair
    - Offer optional solutions
    - If you are unsure, request adjuster's solution

February 7, 19--

Dear Mr. Dolt:

On December 17 our company purchased the X334 Copy
Machine, serial number 513009.

Twice since then, on January 17 and February 2, your service
department repaired the copier.

The copy machine still does not function correctly. Because
our business depends upon prompt communication, it is
extremely important that we have a reliable copier. As a result
of the malfunctioning of the X334, our business has lost 13
hours of usage, which translates into seven hundred dollars
of lost revenue.

We are sure you understand the importance of good business
relationships and wish to maintain your fine reputation. In view
of that, we offer the following suggestion: replace the present
copier with another.

Very truly yours,

Be polite but firm. You wish to cooperate, but your main goal is to correct
a problem. Show patience, but demand prompt action.

Letters of Adjustment

Adjustment letters are responses to the letters of complaint or claim. As
with queries and requests, complaints and claims can be handled in two
ways: granted or refused.

YES — Granting an Adjustment

Composing a letter that grants an adjustment is easy; just say YES!
However, the most important point to remember is that the PRIMARY
purpose of an adjustment letter is to repair damaged customer relations.

How to Repair Damaged Customer Relations

1. First and foremost, say YES! and grant the adjustment.
2. Describe WHAT and WHEN adjustment will be made.
3. Offer explanation of problem or error, if desired.
4. Offer a token gift, if desired.
5. Apologize for any inconvenience.

Dear Mr. Braun:

You have every right to request a replacement for the X334 Copy Machine you purchased.

Our goal is to sell merchandise that is in perfect condition. When a problem develops, we wish to do everything possible to correct it. Our Service Department will remove the first copier and deliver a new one on Monday morning, February twelfth.

We are grateful to you for calling our attention to this model. After further inspection, we have discovered that other X334 copiers of the same shipment were defective, and we are returning them to the manufacturer.

To thank you for your patience, we are including three toner cartridges at our expense. Please accept our sincere apology for any inconvenience this may have caused you. Let us assure you, we will take every precaution in the future that this problem does not occur again!

Very truly yours,

This Letter Granting an Adjustment accomplishes five things:

1. Keeps the customer
2. Mends damaged customer relations
3. Satisfies the customer (THE CUSTOMER IS ALWAYS RIGHT)
4. Creates goodwill
5. Improves your company's reputation

NO — *Refusing an Adjustment*

It's not easy to say NO and keep a customer! Even a compromise with a customer may be viewed as a refusal. This letter requires tact and diplomacy:

- Try to write from the customer's point of view, BUT
- Explain situation from your (adjustor's) point of view.
- Word your letter in a positive way.
- Be <u>agreeable</u> regarding general principles.
- Be <u>cooperative</u> in compromises or partial adjustments.
- Be <u>firm</u> in refusals.
- Appeal to customer to accept evaluation.

Dear Mr. Braun:

Ordinarily you would have every right to request a replacement for the X334 Copy Machine you purchased. Our goal is to sell merchandise that is in perfect condition.

Unfortunately, the machine you purchased on December 17 was part of a special closeout sale, in which all merchandise was tagged, "AS IS. ALL SALES FINAL."

We can understand your frustration with the copier's malfunction, and we have attempted to repair it twice at no cost to you. However, since it was clear at the time of purchase that the machine was in need of repair, we hope you can understand our position, as well.

However, because we value your patronage, we will be happy to repair the copier again at your earliest convenience. Our Service Department will call to make an appointment. We are grateful to you for giving us the opportunity of serving you, our valued customer.

Very truly yours,

This Letter of Refusal of an Adjustment accomplishes four things:

1. Shows company's concern for customer
2. Assures customer of being treated fairly and equitably
3. Improves customer's faith in company's policies
4. Regains customer's business and goodwill

SALES LETTERS OR DIRECT MAILINGS

Sales Letters are often called Direct Mailings. Both are letters mailed to specific groups of people, asking them to buy your product or service. Because these letters can be sent directly to the people most likely to become your customers, they are popular for the following purposes:

- Building product/service name recognition   (Advertising)
- Contacting distant prospects   (More customers)
- Finding leads   (New customers)
- Increasing market share or sales   (More sales)
- Test-marketing new products/services   (New products)

Television and radio advertisements are not very selective means of introducing your product/service to potential customers because ALL groups of people watch TV or listen to the radio. Newspaper, journal, or magazine ads are more selective but are still aimed at general audiences. Direct mailing, however, targets your specific audience. Here's how:

Mailing lists can be bought or rented. Companies specialize in making very specific lists of various groups of people. These lists can be designed according to your needs.

Let's say you wish to sell cosmetics. Which group would most likely contain potential customers?

Male construction workers?	NO
Elementary school children?	NO
Females aged 18–45?	**YES**

Since females aged 18–45 would be the most likely to buy cosmetics, it makes sense to send THEM the letters, and not the others. The selection of groups can be made very precisely. The same group can be further defined for your needs by using additional factors such as skin type, geographical area, climate, educational level, financial status, or any combination of factors.

However, the purpose here is not to decide WHETHER to use prospect lists, but HOW to write direct mailings.

Three factors are needed for successful direct mailings:

1. Product/Service — Must be Excellent
2. Prospect List — Must be Carefully Chosen
3. Sales Letter — Must be WELL Written

IF the product/service is excellent and IF the prospect list is carefully chosen, all that is necessary for success is a well written letter.

Four requirements are essential in a well written sales letter:

1. Get reader's attention
2. Create reader's demand for your product/service
3. Satisfy reader that your product/service is best
4. Call reader to action

This style of writing is called copywriting.

Copywriting

Copywriting requires imagination and flair. Puns and wordplays are eye-catching. One agricultural chemical company needed to attract dairy farmers' attention to their cattle vaccinations. They mailed sales letters with this headline: "THE **HERD** SHOT 'ROUND THE WORLD," a wordplay on the American history saying, "The shot **heard** 'round the world."

GET READER'S ATTENTION

Use clever wording, color, pictures, samples, coupons, gimmicks, but GET THE READER'S ATTENTION. The best advice is to keep the writing EXTREMELY short and entertaining. Remember, the general public's span of attention is measured in seconds.

PRODUCE A DEMAND FOR YOUR PRODUCT/SERVICE

It's known by several names:

- Snob appeal
- Keeping up with the Joneses
- They-got-it-so-I-gotta'-have-it
- If I had ###, I'd be handsome/beautiful/popular/rich/HAPPY

The *Direct Mail Advertising Association* identified twenty-five justifications for people to buy products/services:

To attract the opposite sex	To avoid criticism
To avoid effort	To avoid trouble
To be clean	To be comfortable
To be different	To be like everyone else
To be stylish	To be popular
To make money	To save money
To save time	To preserve possessions
To enjoy	To own beautiful possessions
To be praised	To be healthy
To protect loved ones	To be free from pain
To satisfy curiosity	To appease appetite
To be safe when buying	To protect reputation
To seize the opportunity	

SATISFY READER THAT YOUR PRODUCT/SERVICE IS BEST

Convince the reader QUICKLY that your product/service is the best/fastest/most convenient/most inexpensive/most stylish/most sophisticated/most advanced technologically: *THE BEST!*

For more information, see the **WRITING STYLES FOR LONG REPORTS OR MANUALS** section, particularly the **ANALYSIS** or the **ARGUMENT AND PERSUASION REPORTS** segments. **CHAPTER 18**

CALL READER TO ACTION

This is THE most important part because this is where you get the reader to BUY. Make it sound irresistible and make it sound easy!

Show WHY it's easy

Make it easy for your readers. Make it SOUND easy. Emphasize how simple it is to act NOW.

For more information, see **BUSINESS CORRESPONDENCE OR LETTER WRITING** section, particularly the **MOTIVATING CLOSES** segment. **CHAPTER 13**

RECAP

For your Direct Mailings or your Sales Letters to be successful, remember two issues:

1. YOUR AUDIENCE
2. YOUR PURPOSE

TARGET **your audience, so you have the exact readership you want.**

SELL **your product/service, so you achieve your purpose: success.**

Include these four elements in your letter:

1. Attract attention
2. Create a demand
3. Prove how your product/service is best
4. Call to action

IN-HOUSE MEMOS

AND SHORT REPORTS

15

Three means of written communication in the business world are memos, short reports, and long reports. Memos and short reports are often less formal than long reports, requiring less structure in their writing.

A memo is the updated name for a MEMOrandum. A memorandum is an internal letter or short report sent from one person to another working in the same company. The plural form of memo is memos. The plural form of memorandum is memoranda. Following is a brief formula for writing memos and short reports:

TO:

FROM:

DATE:

RE:

LAYOUT: THE PARTS OF A MEMO OR SHORT REPORT

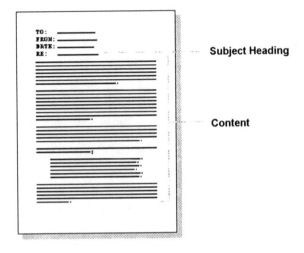

TO:

FROM:

DATE:

RE: (Subject Heading)

- Introduction
- Body of Report
- Conclusion
- Call for Action

The first three parts are easy:

TO: The person(s) for whom the report is written

FROM: Your name; if necessary, your department or company

DATE: Today's date

The fourth part is the one we'll examine:

RE: This means **regarding** or **in regard to** a subject

This is the *subject heading* which "names your aim." It names the topic or identifies your purpose by describing your reason for writing the memo or report. The subject heading is often underlined for emphasis and should be short and concise.

> The same noun that is used in the heading is used later in the introduction to identify your purpose. However, the noun is changed to become a related verb.

Heading:	**Advice** to Staff Regarding 230F Machine Operation	**noun**
Purpose:	To **advise** staff of 230F machine operation....	**verb**
Heading:	**Requisition** of Monthly Meetings	**noun**
Purpose:	To **request** monthly meetings....	**verb**
Heading:	**Authorization** of Subsidiary Purchase	**noun**
Purpose:	To **authorize** purchase of subsidiary....	**verb**

Introduction

Following the subject heading is the *introduction*. It is the first paragraph of the memo or short report. Longer reports may have several paragraphs to introduce the topic.

The introduction of the memo or short report can take four forms:

- Background information
- Consideration of previous report
- Proposal of action
- Criticism of action

PURPOSES OF MEMOS

Background Information

The introductory paragraph describes the past actions or events which have led up to this memo or report. It tells:

- WHY memo or report has been written

  Purpose
- WHAT it is about

  Problem
- HOW it is structured

  Extent
- WHO requested it
- WHEN is its deadline
- WHERE it takes place

The WHY or PURPOSE of a memo or report always uses a strong verb to express its objective. State the PURPOSE in the topic sentence or the first sentence of the paragraph. The following are examples of strong verbs:

...to apprise....

　　...to direct....

　　　　...to evaluate....

　　　　　　...to inform....

　　　　　　　　...to notify....

　　　　　　　　　　...to order....

　　　　　　　　　　　　...to recommend....

　　　　　　　　　　　　　　...to requisition....

　　　　　　　　　　　　　　　　...to survey....

Notice that when stating the purpose, you should always use the infinitive form of the verb: **to** endorse, **to** advise. Follow the topic sentence with support sentences that summarize the action to be taken.

STRONG VERB

SUMMARY OF ACTION TO BE TAKEN

PURPOSE PARAGRAPH

> In *longer reports*, several introductory paragraphs are often necessary to describe the report's purpose, problem situation, and extent or scope of problem.

In *very long reports or manuals*, abstracts may also serve as introductions. These abstracts are summaries which should not be more than 10 percent of the total length of the report.

Consideration of Previous Report

The introductory paragraph refers to a past memo or report. It is a response to an earlier memo or report. Opening phrases can be these:

- ■　In reference to....

- Reference is made to....
- Referring to....
- Proposal of action

Proposal of Action

The introductory paragraph suggests some action or recommendation. It gets right to the point because the subject heading has already informed the reader of the topic. This memo or report needs no background information or point of reference. Opening phrases can be these:

I approve....
> *It is advised....*
>> *The recommendation is (that)....*

Criticism of Action

The introductory paragraph alerts the reader of disapproval. The language is tactful but direct. Opening phrases can be these:

> *It has been brought to my attention (that)....*
> *It has been brought to the VP's notice (that)....*
> *It has been noted (that)....*
> *It has been observed (that)....*

Use the passive voice for criticism. It's much less personal!

Body of Report

Following the introduction is the *body of the report*. It contains all the detailed information that develops the ideas you introduced in the first paragraph(s). These facts further explain or prove your statements.

PRESENT EVIDENCE

Prove your ideas. Be sure each piece of evidence supports your position and serves your purpose. Use one or more of these forms of proof:

- Analogies
- Case histories
- Comparisons/contrasts
- Deductive reasoning—*Logic*
- Definitions

- Examples
- Facts
- Inductive reasoning—*Logic*
- Opinions/testimonies of experts
- Previous Memos
- Reports
- Statistics

For more information, see the **ARGUMENT AND PERSUASION** segment of the **WRITING STYLES FOR LONG REPORTS OR MANUALS** section. **CHAPTER 18**

Conclusion and Call to Action

Following the body of the report is the *conclusion and call to action*. This is the most critical part of any memo or report because it contains the final idea given to the reader.

The closing paragraphs of a memo or report are the most important because those contain the last ideas that will remain with the reader. The end of every memo and report needs two things:

- A Conclusion or Interpretation of the Situation
- A Call to Action

A conclusion summarizes or interprets the material discussed in the memo. Connecting phrases might be these:

Accordingly	Consequently
In conclusion	In view of the situation
Therefore	Thus
To close	To conclude
To review	To recapitulate (OR To recap)
To sum up	To summarize

KINDS OF MEMOS OR APPLYING A CALL TO ACTION

A call to action either asks for support or commands action.
This may occur in one of four ways:

Request	—	Ask ⇨	Weakest of the Four
Suggest	—	Ask ⇨	Fragile but Stronger
Recommend—		Ask ⇨	Strong but Tactful
Command—		**Tell ⇨**	**Bold**

Request

If the call to action is in the form of a REQUEST, it may be phrased in
one of these ways:

> *I would be most appreciative if....*
>
> *It would be appreciated if....*
>
> *We should be most grateful if....*

Suggest

If the call to action is in the form of a SUGGESTION, it might be phrased
in one of these ways:

> *I (would like to) suggest that...be....*
>
> *It is suggested that...be....*
>
> *...could be....*
>
> *...might be....*

Recommend

If the call to action is in the form of a RECOMMENDATION, it could be
phrased in one of the following ways:

> *It is advised that...be....*
>
> *It is advisable to....*
>
> *It is believed that...should (be)....*
>
> *It is doubted that...should (be)....*
>
> *It is recommended that...be....*
>
> *We (would like to) recommend (that)...be....*

Command

If the call to action is in the form of a COMMAND, it may be phrased in one of the following ways:

> *Please confirm that...is/are....*
>
> *...is/are to (be)....*
>
> *...must (be)....*

Remember, the call to action is the place where you state your case, where you ask for what you want. This is THE most important part of any memo or report, whether short or long.

Whichever form you choose, be sure the call to action makes these three most important things clear:

WHO should do it ⇨ PERFORMER

WHAT he/she should do ⇨ ACTION

WHEN he/she should do it ⇨ DEADLINE

The stronger the directions of the call to action, the more effective the memo or report!

Memos and short reports are popular ways of communicating information. However, the formal or long report, although more complex, is often the preferred approach because it is the most convincing.

When writing long reports or manuals, follow the guidelines for organizing and presenting material that are offered in the following chapters.

Long Reports and Manuals

or Planning Guidelines

1. Select topic and limit scope
2. Brainstorm
3. List sources of information (AKA Bibliography)
4. Note pieces of information
5. Organize information or classy classification
6. Limn or outline long reports/manuals
7. Write rough draft
8. Edit several times
   - For information errors or omissions (by you)
   - For information errors or omissions (by others)
   - For punctuation errors
   - For syntax or grammatical errors
   - For spelling errors
   - For typos or typographical errors
9. Rewrite
10. Assemble final Bibliography
11. Create Table of Contents with page numbers

SELECT TOPIC AND LIMIT SCOPE

Selection of topic is usually decided for you. However, if you need help generating ideas, try Free-Writing or Spread-Sheet Writing.

Limiting of scope is also an important part of writing. If the range is too wide, you will either have to write books and **books** and more **books** of material, or you will only be able to write in a general way about vague stereotypes.

Your best bet is to limit your subject by writing about one small area. Write THOROUGHLY but specifically about one aspect. Remember, don't write about the whole pie; write about one slice.

See the **GENERATING IDEAS** section for both selection and limitation of topics. **CHAPTER 5**

BRAINSTORM

Work with others to develop ideas for your report. Set aside an hour or two for a Think-Tank session with colleagues. Remember, two heads are better than one; three are better than two.

LIST SOURCES OF INFORMATION

Keep a record of all sources and resources. If you find data in a particular memo or journal, write down not only the information, but also the name, number, volume, or date. If you interview an authority, record the date, name, organization.

In a formal report or manual, the information sources must be listed in a bibliography at the end of the report.

NOTE RANDOM PIECES OF INFORMATION

Keep accurate records of **ALL** bits of information. Details are easily misplaced if not filed in an orderly fashion. A notebook specifically used for that report, and that report only, is the most effective way to keep track of miscellaneous notes.

ORGANIZE INFORMATION OR CLASSY CLASSIFICATION

Follow these six steps to classifying information:

1. Record miscellaneous notes in first notebook
2. Determine classifications
   - Begin classifying the various parts of your report now
   - Assign different divisions for the information

3. Divide second notebook into classifications

   - Start a second notebook

   - Divide it into the various classifications

4. Transfer information from first into second notebook

   - Begin entering the information from your first notebook into the second

5. Arrange material according to classification

   - Record material according to classification

6. Cross off areas of first book as you transfer material

   - As you move information between the books, cross out the material originally recorded in the first notebook

   - When no unmarked areas remain in the first book, the information is completely organized in the second

LIMN OR OUTLINE LONG REPORTS/MANUALS

Arrange ideas in a logical order

Arrange ideas to help readers follow your thoughts

For more information, refer to the **ARRANGING IDEAS EFFECTIVELY OR LIMNING** section. **CHAPTER 6**

WRITE ROUGH DRAFT

YOUR JOB: JUST WRITE

Using your sketch of ideas (or outline) to guide you, write the first draft of your report. Just write. Don't criticize or judge. Your thoughts will flow more smoothly if you don't stop to edit. DON'T WORRY about punctuation, grammar, spelling, or typos—YET.

EDIT SEVERAL TIMES

YOUR JOB: NOW CHECK FOR ERRORS

Editing is THE most important part of writing. Reports are never letter-perfect in the rough draft, so proofreading is critical. Proofread to FIND the errors. Then edit to CORRECT the errors.

- **WRITING** is your job during the rough draft phase.
- **EDITING** is your job during the editing phase.

Editing Strategies

Correcting on a computer seems easier than correcting by hand, but both have their advantages and disadvantages.

COMPUTER EDITING

When correcting on a computer, changes may be typed directly into the text, which saves time. However, there are two drawbacks.

- Exchanging disks with coworkers is awkward. Disks can be lost, or files can be erased accidentally.

- Recording editorial changes is difficult. New files must be created and renamed constantly. Because the process can be confusing, it increases errors.

LONGHAND EDITING

Editing by hand on a hard-copy printout is the best method. Although corrections have to be retyped later, the extra time and strokes are worth the advantages.

By working from a printout, mistakes are easier to spot, both by you and others. Each editor can make corrections by using a different colored ink. These corrections can then be reexamined by all concerned. Later these suggestions and corrections can either be added or omitted in the final draft of the report.

EDITING ON A PRINTOUT

- Mistakes are easily located
- Corrections are made by each editor
- Corrections are color-coded to each editor
- **ALL** editors can **REVIEW** all suggested corrections
- Suggested corrections can be included or not

Editing Levels

Editing should be done at many levels.
At each level, search for ONE KIND of mistake only.

1. Edit for information errors or omissions.
    - Is your data correct?
    - Have you forgotten some important point?

2. Have other experts double-check for errors or omissions.
    - Can others find incorrect data?
    - Can others find points you've forgotten?

3. Check for punctuation errors.

4. Check for syntax or grammatical errors.
    - Is the word order correct?
    - Do verbs, nouns, and pronouns agree?

5. Check for spelling errors.
    - Use a spell-checker on the computer.
    - Keep a dictionary at hand.

6. Check for typing errors (typos).

REWRITE

Decide which of the suggested additions, corrections, and changes improve your report. Add them to your first rough draft. Rewrite. Use the thesaurus for variety of expression. Edit again for spelling, punctuation, grammatical, or typing errors. Now polish: go over *and over **and over*** the report until it's letter-perfect.

- Add editorial changes to rough draft
- Rewrite
- Use thesaurus
- Edit AGAIN!
- Polish

For more information, see the **EDITING, REWRITING, AND POLISHING** section. **CHAPTER 19**

ASSEMBLE FINAL BIBLIOGRAPHY

List all sources of reference:

- Articles from journals or magazines
- Books
- Interviews
- Memos
- Newspapers
- Television or radio broadcasts
- Videos

By listing every source you have used, you do two things:

1. Provide additional reference material for your readers
2. Increase the credibility
   - of yourself
   - of your report

The bibliography appears on the last page of a long report or manual. In a FORMAL report or manual, it is important to observe the stylistic conventions or form. The following is based on the MLA format of documentation (Gibaldi and Achtert 94–12):

Divide each entry or record into three parts:

Part 1   1) **Authors' name(s)**

Last names first

Part 2   2) **Titles**

Underline titles of books

Underline titles of magazines

Enclose titles of articles in quotation marks

Part 3   3) **Publication information of sources**

Books:

Place of publication

Publisher

Year of publication

Magazines:

Volume and page numbers

Date

Each of the three parts ends with a PERIOD.

STYLE:

- Top margin — 2"
- Other margins — 1"
- Additional lines — indent five more spaces

Book:

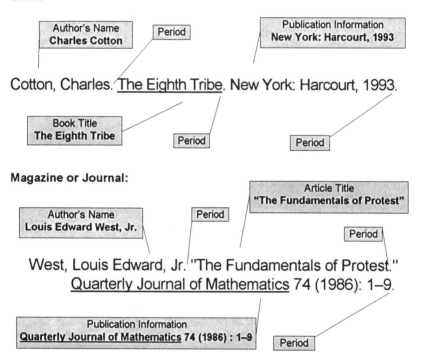

Cotton, Charles. The Eighth Tribe. New York: Harcourt, 1993.

Magazine or Journal:

West, Louis Edward, Jr. "The Fundamentals of Protest." Quarterly Journal of Mathematics 74 (1986): 1–9.

CREATE TABLE OF CONTENTS

Although not necessary with a short report, a table of contents is a helpful addition to long reports and is a necessity for manuals. Placed at the front of the report or manual, after the title page, the table of contents lists the various divisions and their page numbers. This is useful for finding information quickly.

OPTIONAL PARTS OF A LONG REPORT OR MANUAL

This optional section is to be used
FOR REFERENCE <u>ONLY</u>.

Very few reports—IF ANY—use all of these parts!

Depending upon their purpose and audience, long reports and manuals can have various parts or components, for example:

1. Scientific or architectural reports often have abstracts that appear at the beginning, but other fields don't allow this.

2. Only the longest, most formal reports or manuals contain tables of contents or bibliographies.

3. Appendixes are an option, not a necessity.

Long reports and manuals MAY contain the following elements.

Optional Elements of a Report

Abstract—*A summary of the main topics or aspects of report*

Title page—*Contains complete title, subtitle, author's name*

Table of contents—*Contains listing of divisions and their page numbers*

Letter of transference—*Letter to recipient of report*

Statement of purpose—*Reason for writing report*

Scope or limitation—*States depth of report or parameters*

Subheadings and subdivisions—*Titles of report's sections*

Numbered paragraphs—*Paragraphs are identified by numbers*

Proposal—*Proposition or recommendation*

Method(s)—*Style or manner in which report was written*

Conclusion—*Summary of topics reported*

Call to action—*Request for support or action*

Bibliography—*List of references used*

Appendix(es)—*Diagrams, graphs, charts*

REPORTS' TONE:

LEVELS OF FORMALITY

It's not so much what you say...

...as how you say it.

When writing a report, you already know the following:

- Subject must be clear to both YOU and YOUR READER.
  - Words must **quickly** and **precisely** describe situation.
  - Words must **quickly** and **precisely** recommend action.
- Information must be well organized.
  - Data must be easy to understand.
- Wording must be concise—the fewer words, the better.
- Sentences must be easy to understand—short sentences.
- Emphasis can be achieved by PLACEMENT and AMOUNT OF AREA.

The next areas to examine are tone and the levels of formality.

Just as relationships differ in your personal life, relationships vary in your professional life. Associations between YOU, the writer, and your readers are reflected in the use of different tones and levels of formality.

Word Choice

Your choice of words is the most important influence of tone and level of formality. However, six factors determine the proper degree of formality in your writing:

1. Language
2. Contractions
3. Abbreviations
4. Personal Pronouns
5. Passive Voice (In Moderation)
6. Your Audience

LANGUAGE

A casual memo will use informal expressions, while a formal report will use more sophisticated language. Long reports and manuals usually require a more dignified vocabulary.

The lower the level of formality, the more conversational the tone. The higher the level of formality, the more business-like the tone. Formal reports demand more formal language.

INFORMAL	FORMAL
so-so	satisfactory
got better and better	improved
got worse and worse	depreciated; declined
lots of	multiple; recurrently
not a lot	few; occasional
keep in touch	keep apprised; keep informed

CONTRACTIONS

Avoid contractions. Write entire words.

INFORMAL	FORMAL
aren't	are not
she's	she is; she has

ABBREVIATIONS

Avoid abbreviations. Write entire words.

INFORMAL	FORMAL
Dept.	Department
Corp.	Corporation

PERSONAL PRONOUNS

Avoid personal pronouns. The more formal the language, the less personal it should be. To be less personal (as in a long report or manual), omit personal pronouns: *I, WE, OUR, US, YOU, YOUR.* Instead, use impersonal terms that are "colder," more detached. This creates more distance between YOU, the writer, and your topic of conversation.

PERSONAL	IMPERSONAL OR IMPARTIAL
our idea	the company's proposal
we wanted	the corporation required
your letter to us	the correspondence received

PASSIVE VOICE (In Moderation)

If ever a time for the passive voice were needed, this is it. The passive voice is **extremely** impersonal. The message seems written by a fax machine instead of a person.

The passive voice directs the readers' attention to the contents of the message—not to the author.

YOUR AUDIENCE

Words reflect relationships between people. You wouldn't use the same tone of voice in speaking to your employer as in speaking to your employee. The situation is the same in writing. Whether spoken or written, WORDS indicate the relationship between people.

Remember your audience!

Your audience is made up of three groups of people: **superiors, colleagues** or coworkers, and **subordinates.** Your tone reflects your position in relation to the readers.

The direction of your tone is up, sideways (lateral), or down.

SUPERIORS	—	↑ UP	—	RESPECT
COLLEAGUES	—	→ LATERAL	—	COURTESY
SUBORDINATES	—	↓ DOWN	—	AUTHORITY

- ■ Be respectful with superiors.
- ■ Be courteous with colleagues.
- ■ Be authoritative with subordinates.

- ■ When writing to your *manager*, your tone is more respectful, more submissive.
- ■ When writing to a member of your *staff*, your tone becomes more authoritative, more dominant.
- ■ Your tone for *coworkers* falls somewhere in the middle.

RESPECTFUL	AUTHORITATIVE
could be	is
should be	is
would be	will
might/may	will
seems to be	is
looks as if	is
appears	is
almost decided	decided
about certain	certain
firmer	firm
more secure	secure

Your relationship with the reader also determines how you phrase questions. The higher the position of your reader, the more respectful the tone. The lower the business rank of the reader, the more commanding the tone.

SP	1.	*I would be most appreciative of your signature.*
SP	2.	*Would it be at all possible to have your signature?*
C	3.	*Could you please sign this?*
C	4.	*Would you add your signature to this?*
SB	5.	*Please sign.*

(**SP**) Numbers one and two would be used in writing to a superior.

(**C**) Numbers three and four would be courteous, as for a colleague.

(**SB**) Number five is a directive to a subordinate.

WRITING STYLES

FOR LONG REPORTS OR MANUALS

In the world of business, writing long reports or manuals is **EITHER** a necessary evil, **OR** it's the most effective medium you have for expressing your ideas and goals. It depends upon your viewpoint.

Once you feel comfortable with writing, long reports or manuals give you the opportunity to state your opinions. You can show your skills to the decision-makers in your organization. All the tools you need are at your fingertips for advancing your ideas and promoting yourself.

These writing styles are best suited to long reports or manuals:

1. Comparison/Contrast—To compare various ideas or choices

2. Process—To instruct readers in step-by-step procedures

3. Analysis—To analyze various strategies, choices

4. Description—To inform organizations of specific data

5. Argument and Persuasion—To convince readers

COMPARISON/CONTRAST

Comparison = Similarities

A Comparison report COMPARES two subjects that are similar.

A Comparison of two subjects shows their similarities.

Contrast = Differences

A Contrast report CONTRASTS two subjects that are different.

A Contrast of two subjects shows their differences.

A Comparison/Contrast report may be organized in two ways:

■ aspect-by-aspect

■ subject-by-subject.

Aspect-by-Aspect

When organizing aspect-by-aspect, the writer compares the similarities or contrasts the differences, one-by-one, *alternating* back and forth between the subjects.

Subject-by-Subject

When organizing subject-by-subject, the writer compares or contrasts *first* one subject's, *then* the other subject's, similarities or differences.

STYLE 1		STYLE 2
Aspect-by-Aspect		**Subject-by-Subject**
Dragons vs. TIGERS		*Dragons* vs. TIGERS
	Paragraph #	
Introduction & a,b,c	1	Introduction & a,b,c
a re: *Dragons*	2	a re: *Dragons*
a re: **TIGERS**	3	b re: *Dragons*
b re: *Dragons*	4	c re: *Dragons*
b re: **TIGERS**	5	a re: **TIGERS**
c re: *Dragons*	6	**b** re: **TIGERS**
c re: **TIGERS**	7	**c** re: **TIGERS**
Conclusion	8	Conclusion

Style One of Comparison/Contrast

Using the aspect-by-aspect approach of Style 1, compare or contrast your subjects, one point at a time.

INTRODUCTION

After an introduction, mention the way in which you will present your topics. Announce that you will compare them point-by-point or aspect-by-aspect. This will alert your readers for what's to come. Briefly mention the points or aspects that you will be examining.

TELL THEM WHAT YOU ARE GOING TO TELL THEM

TELL THEM

TELL THEM WHAT YOU TOLD THEM

For a gradual increase of evidence, it is best to start comparing/contrasting with the weakest point and build up to the strongest point. That way, your work will be done for you. The audience will be convinced by the material. Your conclusion will only confirm their growing belief.

BODY OF REPORT

The body of the report contains the information that you will give your readers.

TELL THEM WHAT YOU ARE GOING TO TELL THEM

TELL THEM

TELL THEM WHAT YOU TOLD THEM

In the first paragraph of the report's body, describe one point of one subject. In the second paragraph of the report's body, describe the same point, but of the *other* subject. In other words, *alternate* back and forth between the two subjects.

For instance, let's say you are comparing the two subjects, rice and noodles. Your *first* point or aspect is the fact that they are both carbohydrates. This is what the first two paragraphs of the report's body might look like:

> *1. Rice is a natural form of carbohydrates, with the nutrition going directly from the plant into the digestive system. The whole pearls of rice retain all their nutrients.*

> *2. Noodles are an excellent form of carbohydrates. Although processed, and thereby losing some of their nutritional benefits, they allow the remaining nutrients to be more readily absorbed by the digestive system.*

1. In the first paragraph, you discuss how **rice** is a carbohydrate. The subject is rice; the aspect is carbohydrate.

2. In the second paragraph, you discuss how noodles are carbohydrates. The subject is noodles; the aspect is carbohydrate.

   In the next two paragraphs, you compare/contrast the *second* aspect:

3. In paragraph three, you discuss how rice is one form of fiber.

4. In paragraph four, you discuss how noodles are another form of fiber.

   In the following two paragraphs, compare/contrast the *third* aspect:

5. In paragraph five, you discuss the economics of rice.

6. In paragraph six, you discuss the economics of noodles.

You may use as many paragraphs as are needed for each subject and each aspect. A MINIMUM of one paragraph for each subject and each aspect is necessary.

Continue comparing/contrasting the subjects, aspect-by-aspect, *alternating from the first subject to the second*, until you have discussed all the points.

This is what STYLE 1 of a Comparison/Contrast report looks like:

Introduction		*paragraph 1*
Rice	—aspect 1—carbohydrates	*paragraph 2*
Noodles	—aspect 1—carbohydrates	*paragraph 3*
Rice	—aspect 2—fiber	*paragraph 4*
Noodles	—aspect 2—fiber	*paragraph 5*
Rice	—aspect 3—economics	*paragraph 6*
Noodles	—aspect 3—economics	*paragraph 7*
Rice	—aspect 4—?	*paragraph 8*
Noodles	—aspect 4—?	*paragraph 9*
Conclusion and Call to Action		*paragraph 10*

CONCLUSION

Conclude your report by reviewing all the aspects. In your summary, explain how one subject or the other is better because of the points or aspects already mentioned. Now call your readers to action, based upon the facts of your report.

TELL THEM WHAT YOU ARE GOING TO TELL THEM

TELL THEM

TELL THEM WHAT YOU TOLD THEM

CALL TO ACTION

That final step, *the call to action*, is the most powerful means you have for getting results. Because your objective is disguised as a suggestion or recommendation, your readers are more willing to agree to your request.

Write persuasively. If your points build to a climax, from the weakest to the strongest, you gradually convince your readers with facts. By allowing them to form "their own" conclusions, you win their support. Your summary only strengthens their growing belief. Now your call to action persuades them to help you.

How to Influence Readers

- Write persuasively
- Progress from weakest to strongest points
- Allow readers to form "their own" conclusions
- Summarize to reinforce "their" belief (your own)
- CALL READERS TO ACTION

Style Two of Comparison/Contrast

Using the subject-by-subject approach of Style 2, you compare/contrast your subjects by *first* listing all the aspects of one subject, and *then* listing all the aspects of the other subject.

INTRODUCTION

After an introduction, mention the manner in which you will present your topics. Announce that you will be comparing all the points or aspects of the first subject, and then all the points or aspects of the second subject. This will alert your readers of your system. Briefly mention the points or aspects that you will be comparing/contrasting.

For a gradual increase of evidence, it is best to start comparing/contrasting with the weakest point and build up to the strongest point. That way, your work will be done for you. The audience will be convinced by the material. Your conclusion will only confirm their growing belief.

BODY OF REPORT

The body of the report contains the information for your readers.

In the first paragraph of the report's body, describe one point of one subject. In the second paragraph of the report's body, describe the second point of the SAME subject.

For instance, let's say you are comparing the two subjects, rice and noodles. Your first point or aspect is the fact that they are both carbohydrates. The second point is that they both contain fiber. This is what the first two paragraphs of the report's body might look like:

> *Rice is a natural form of carbohydrate, with the nutrition going directly from the plant into the digestive system. The whole pearls of rice retain all their nutrients.*

> *Rice is an excellent source of fiber. What our grandmothers called "roughage" is what today's nutritionists are calling fiber.*

In the following paragraphs, compare/contrast ALL THE ASPECTS of the *first* subject. When you are finished describing the first subject completely, begin writing about the second subject.

Paragraph by paragraph, list ALL THE ASPECTS of the *second* subject.

Keep subjects parallel. List both subjects' aspects in the same sequence or order. For instance, if the *first subject's aspects* are listed as 1) carbohydrates, 2) fiber, and 3) economics, make sure that the *second subject's aspects* are listed in the same way.

You may use as many paragraphs as are needed for each subject and each aspect. A MINIMUM of one paragraph for each subject and each aspect is necessary.

CONCLUSION

Conclude your report by restating all the aspects, FIRST OF ONE and then of THE SECOND SUBJECT. In your summary, stress why one subject or the other is better because of the points or aspects already mentioned. Now call your readers to action, based upon the facts of your report.

This is what STYLE 2 of a Comparison/Contrast report looks like:

Introduction   *paragraph 1*

Rice	—aspect 1—carbohydrates	*paragraph 2*
Rice	—aspect 2—fiber	*paragraph 3*
Rice	—aspect 3—economics	*paragraph 4*
Rice	—aspect 4—?	*paragraph 5*
Noodles	—aspect 1—carbohydrates	*paragraph 6*
Noodles	—aspect 2—fiber	*paragraph 7*
Noodles	—aspect 3—economics	*paragraph 8*
Noodles	—aspect 4—?	*paragraph 9*

Conclusion and Call to Action   *paragraph 10*

PROCESS

A Process report explains how to do something.
It is a step-by-step procedure.

Process = How To

Process

Paragraph #	Directions (using Time Transitions)
1.	Introduction OR Statement of Purpose
2.	First....
3.	Do not (forget to)...[insert any warning here].
4.	Second....
5.	Then....
6.	After....
7.	Next....
8.	Finally....
9.	Conclusion

A Process report:

- gives directions
- gives guidance
- tells HOW TO
- explains

Use the process style of writing whenever directions include a series of steps. For policies and procedures to be consistently carried out, give clear directions that are easy to follow.

INTRODUCTION

As with every type of report, begin with an opening paragraph that introduces your subject. Briefly mention what process you will be describing. Then state your purpose; tell why you are writing this report.

- Tell WHAT
- Tell WHY

BODY OF REPORT

THINK

Before you start listing instructions, mentally go through the process or procedure you are going to describe. What must the readers know before they can begin? What is the next thing? Then what? But what if that situation exists? Then what do they do?

LIST

After you have thought of every possible problem or exception, list every step necessary to perform the process.

Tell **HOW**

ARRANGE

THE MORE LOGICAL, THE MORE EFFECTIVE

Arrange the steps in the most logical order. The easier the report is to read, the more often the process will be performed correctly.

SIMPLIFY

THE CLEARER, THE BETTER

Use only one paragraph for each instruction. If there are various features of a particular instruction, use a separate paragraph for each feature. Make it clear. Make it easy to follow.

INCLUDE WARNINGS

If there are any areas the readers should be warned about, mention the areas BEFORE the readers encounter them. Don't tell them to wear electrical gloves AFTER you've instructed them to touch live electrical wires.

USE "TIME" WORDS

Tell **WHEN**

Time transitions are words like "first," "second," "then," and "next." Use them to further illustrate the ORDER of the process.

Time Transitions

after	at the present time	at the same time
at this point	before	during
eventually	finally	first (second)
further	hence	henceforth
in time	in due time	later
meanwhile	next	once
secondly	since	sooner or later
then	until	until now
when	whenever	

Describe the last step with a word or phrase like finally, end by, or in conclusion.

CONCLUSION

Again state your purpose in writing the process report. Summarize the steps involved in performing the process. Call the readers to action.

- Restate purpose
- Summarize steps
- Call to action

TRANSITIONS

Some transitional words and phrases are better than others at signalling a summary of ideas or a final restatement of topic ideas:

as a result	as can be seen	as shown above
consequently	for these reasons	for this reason
generally speaking	hence	in any case
in any event	in brief	in conclusion
in either case	in fact	in other words
in summary	on the whole	therefore
thus	to sum up	

CALL TO ACTION

That final step, the call to action, is the most powerful means you have for getting the results you want. Because your objective is disguised as a suggestion or recommendation, your readers are more willing to follow your directions.

EXERCISE I FOR PROCESS—TEA BREWING

Match the words in Column A with the directions in Column B to make a cup of tea:

COLUMN A	COLUMN B
FIRST	Pour the tea into the teacup
SECOND	Pour the milk into the teacup
NEXT	Leave the teapot
AFTER THAT	Fill the tea kettle with water
THEN	Put some tea into the teapot
NEXT	Boil the water
AFTER THIS	Warm the teapot for a while
FINALLY	Fill teapot with boiling water

ANALYSIS

Analysis is sometimes called interpretation. It is the division of a whole into its parts to find the underlying meaning. However, there can be many different interpretations, so the writer must use proof to convince the reader of one particular interpretation's logic or truth.

Analytical reports are written to examine different tactics or choices. Analysis is a means of simplifying. It divides the whole into its parts. In effect, it makes the difficult easy.

The role of the analyst—YOU—is to think of the various features of a subject and how they relate to each other. Your job is to explain the material, organize it for easy reading by the audience, and recommend action.

- Interpret information
- Organize
- Recommend action

Analytical Thought Process

The steps you will use to interpret the information, organize it, and recommend action are listed in the following process:

1. Consider the whole from all aspects, all viewpoints.
2. What patterns do you see?
3. These repeating patterns are the parts of the whole.
4. Focus on these patterns or parts.
5. Arrange similar patterns into groups.
6. How do these groups connect with each other?
7. Are there features which don't fit into these groups?
8. Find new patterns among these and arrange into groups.
9. How are all these patterns connected to the whole?
10. Base conclusion on the following:

    a) How the whole is divided into the parts.

    b) How the parts are connected.

    c) How the parts create the whole.

After you've analyzed the material, organize the material into a writing format, a formula:

Analysis Report Structure

1. **Introduction**

   (Include reasoning for groupings)

2. **Body of Report**

   Pattern grouping
   Examples
   Pattern grouping
   Examples
   Pattern grouping
   Examples
   Pattern grouping
   Examples
   Pattern grouping
   Examples
   Pattern grouping
   Examples

3. **Conclusion**

   (Include summary of patterns)
   (Include Call to Action)

INTRODUCTION

As with every type of report, begin with an opening paragraph or two that introduce your subject. Briefly mention your logic for classification or grouping. Then state your reasons for choosing these particular patterns. Show the purposes for these; tell HOW these groupings will evaluate the subject. Finally state your purpose; tell WHY you are writing this report.

  a) Introduce subject
  b) Describe basis for classification
  c) Explain WHY you chose these patterns
  d) Tell HOW these groups measure the subject
  e) State WHY you are writing this report

BODY OF REPORT

Arrange your pattern groupings in the order that will best serve your purposes. By creating an arrangement that builds toward your goal, you gently influence the readers.

  a) Arrange weakest points first
  b) Build to strongest point

Begin a new paragraph for each pattern grouping, each classification. Explain your reasons for choosing that particular pattern. Describe how it helps examine the subject, how that part relates to the whole.

After discussing the first pattern grouping or classification, begin a new paragraph. In it, list the examples of that pattern. Explain how they represent that pattern. Show how the parts fit together to create the whole.

  a) Begin a new paragraph for every pattern grouping
  b) Explain reasons for choosing each pattern
  c) Describe HOW each uniquely examines the subject
  d) Describe HOW each part relates to the whole

Transitions and Connectives

When listing examples, some transitional words and phrases are better than others at signaling the reader:

as	for example	for instance
in fact	in general	such as

Keep the paragraphs flowing smoothly from each sentence to the next with the use of connectives. Do not **over**use these words and phrases, for that would slow down the pace of your writing. However, cautious use of them will guide your readers from sentence to sentence, idea to idea:

also	another	as a result	at last
consequently	finally	first (second)	for instance
furthermore	for this purpose	likewise	next
otherwise	on the contrary	similarly	such
then	on the other hand	thus	

You may use as many paragraphs as needed for each pattern grouping and each listing of examples. A MINIMUM of one paragraph for each classification and each set of examples is necessary.

Create new paragraphs for every pattern group and every set of examples until you have used them all. Arrange the classifications from the weakest to the strongest. Build toward your goal.

CONCLUSION

End with a summary of the main patterns and an explanation of the analysis. Based on the *evidence* of the analysis, recommend an action or choice. Based on the *conclusion* of your analysis, call your audience to action.

a) Summarize main patterns
b) Comment on analysis
c) Recommend action or choice
d) Call to action

DESCRIPTION

Descriptive writing involves close examination of details, first by you, and then by your readers. Through concrete, clear, specific description, allow your readers to visualize a subject—through your eyes. Allow them to *see* your point of view.

THINGS ARE CONCRETE. IDEAS ARE ABSTRACT.

SHOW, DON'T TELL!

The advice for keeping your writing concrete: SHOW, DON'T TELL! If you describe something well to your readers, you show them. They can *see* it. If you only tell about it, they cannot get a clear picture.

Learn to recognize **Showing** versus **Telling**:

Telling:

> *Everyone stopped talking as a tall woman walked into the room.*

Showing:

> *The wedding party gasped, as if on cue. Conversations ceased as the blond, Nordic beauty gracefully swept all six foot-two inches of herself into the gilded ballroom.*

PERSUASION AND INFLUENCE CHANGE THE RULES

Occasionally when writing descriptive reports, your goal is not only to describe, but also to PERSUADE or INFLUENCE your audience. In this case, you may WANT your writing slanted so your readers will be more likely to accept your ideas.

The passive voice is useful when you WANT the writing to appear vague. If, for example, you don't want the readers to know WHO decided to lower the salaries, use the passive voice.

By being specific, you increase your credibility because you prove your points as you write. Use facts to avoid confusion. Use facts to convince your readers that your ideas make sense.

> For more information, refer to the **WRITING STRATEGIES** section.
> **CHAPTER 1**

Connectives and Transitions

As with all styles of report writing, transitions help to move one idea toward the next. Keep the paragraphs flowing smoothly from each sentence to the next with the use of connectives.

Do not **over**use these words and phrases, for that would slow down the pace of your writing. However, cautious use of them will guide your readers from sentence to sentence, idea to idea.

Descriptive paragraphs often arrange items or ideas in SPACE:

Spatial transitions restrict or limit **space**:

above	across from	adjacent to	also
before me	below	beyond	further
here	in the distance	nearby	next to
on the left	on the right	opposite to	there
to the left	to the right	where	wherever

Sometimes descriptive paragraphs arrange items or ideas in TIME:

Time transitions restrict or limit **time**:

after	at the present time	at the same time
at this point	before	during
eventually	finally	first (second)
further	hence	henceforth
in time	in due time	later
meanwhile	next	once
secondly	since	sooner or later
then	until	until now
when	whenever	

FORMULA FOR DESCRIPTIVE REPORTS

1. Introduction

      (With preview of topics to be described)

2. Body of Report

      a) First Topic

      b) Second Topic

      c) Third Topic

3. Conclusion

      (With summary of topics described)

      (With call to action)

ARGUMENT AND PERSUASION

Argument and persuasion are both forms of writing that attempt to convince readers. Although similar to each other, they have a basic difference in their tones. Argument uses a rational, logical appeal to the intellect. Persuasion uses a more emotional appeal. Often the two styles are combined.

- Argument—Appeals to the Intellect
- Persuasion—Appeals to the Emotions

The Six Elements

Six elements are essential to good argument and persuasion:

1. Analyze and clearly present facts
2. Propose solution
3. Support with evidence, proof
4. Answer and disprove opposing views
5. Restate your position in conclusion
6. Call to action

THE STRUCTURE OF ARGUMENT

In developing an argument, the following format can help you limn or outline your report by letting you see the cause-and-effect relationship between your proposal and your evidence. As with all reports, there's a beginning, a middle, and an ending: an introduction, a body of the argument, and a conclusion.

Introduction

The introduction may contain one or several paragraphs and should include the following features:

Opening statements

Opening statements are attention-getters that gain readers' support immediately. Use one of these:

- Anecdote — human-interest story
- Personal reference — personal experience
- Description — word "picture"
- Background — description or explanation of history
- Proposal — issue that is to be proven or defended
- Brief list of topics — introduction of the points discussed in the body of the Argument

Body of the Argument

Present evidence

Use facts to prove your argument. Be sure each piece of evidence is closely connected to your reasoning. Only use information that's important to your argument. Use these forms of proof:

- Analogies
- Case histories
- Comparisons/contrasts
- Deductive reasoning   *(Logic)*
- Definitions
- Examples

- Facts
- Inductive reasoning   *(Logic)*
- Memos
- Opinions/testimonies of experts
- Reports
- Statistics

> **Your goal is to convince your readers that your proposal is the right one. Respect your opponents' views. Admit their good points. Then show why your proposal makes more sense, why your proposal is better. Always end with your strongest point or your best argument. This makes your case more convincing.**

Disprove opposing views

Answer or refute all arguments against your proposal; don't ignore them.

- List each one and prove how it is false, unclear, contradictory, or illogical.
- Rely on facts and reason—instead of emotion—to demonstrate HOW **your** proposal is better.

Concede

If an opposing argument has a good point, say so! Graciously admit it. By demonstrating that you have studied all sides of the argument, you gain face. You gain your readers' respect and confidence. By making a concession, you show you are reasonable.

Now show WHY **your** proposal is better.

> **Sometimes a concession is made at the beginning of a report. Consider your audience. Decide if an earlier placement will decrease opposition and gain support for you. Americans have a saying: An ounce of prevention is worth a pound of cure.**

Conclusion

Summarize

- Review your main arguments
- Restate your proposal's reasoning

Call to action

- Ask for your readers' support

ASK FOR WHAT **YOU** WANT!

EDITING, REWRITING, AND POLISHING 19

Editing is a lot like carving ice. Your rough draft is a cold block of ice that you need to carve and smooth until it becomes a graceful sculpture.

Pause Before Examining

To begin editing, step back for an overview. Let some distance develop between YOU and your writing. Wait several days before editing to allow yourself to be objective.

Time = Distance

After several days, look closely at your work. Examine every facet, every detail.

Read Out Loud

Read your writing out loud. HEARING it helps to find your mistakes.

THE INVISIBLE WRITING SYSTEM OF EDITING

The purpose of editing is to make your writing become invisible. You want your audience to understand your ideas, NOT look at your writing style. To do that, your writing must be so perfect that it disappears.

When editing, rewriting, and polishing, follow this process:

1) PARAGRAPHS

- Develop strong topic sentences
- Arrange progression of paragraphs from weak to strong
- Make sure report has a conclusion
- Make sure each paragraph has a conclusion
- Use specific details to support topic sentences
- Leave out unrelated sentences OR begin new paragraphs
- Use transitions

2) SENTENCES

- Keep sentences short
- Vary sentence structures
- Combine sentences
- Have concluding sentence

3) TECHNIQUE

- Be objective—not subjective
- Tone—consider your word choice
- Place words correctly for emphasis
- Place ideas correctly for emphasis
- Use active—not passive—voice
- Be concise

4) NUTS AND BOLTS

- Check for errors or omissions
- Check for spelling
- Check for punctuation
- Check for grammar
- Check for typos (typographical errors)

Paragraphs

STRONG TOPIC SENTENCES

Let's review the construction of a report:

Introduction	—	Statement of purpose
Body of report	—	First subject
	—	Second subject
	—	Third subject
Conclusion	—	Restatement of purpose

TOPIC SENTENCE—Within the body of the report, every subject has at least one paragraph to describe its idea. A topic sentence is usually but not always the first sentence of each paragraph. A topic sentence does two things:

1. Describes the contents of the paragraph
2. Supports the introduction's statement of purpose

The topic sentence of each paragraph signals the direction of your report to the audience. Rewrite the topic sentence until it expresses your idea exactly. Unless it properly describes the paragraph's content and strengthens the report's purpose, it will confuse your audience.

Make sure the topic sentence clearly does two things:

- **DESCRIBES** paragraph
- **SUPPORTS** your report's purpose

EXERCISE FOR DESCRIPTIVE TOPIC SENTENCE

Following is a paragraph which contains supporting sentences and a concluding sentence. Write a descriptive topic sentence for it.

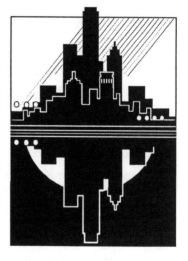

Air pollution is at record levels. Traffic jams are common. Rush hour is a disaster. The cars are backed-up for miles. Road intersections are gridlocked; cars can't cross the street in either direction. Parking is even worse. Parking space was not a consideration in the construction of the city. This boom town was unprepared for such fast growth. With too many cars already, no other automobiles should be allowed in the city.

_____

_____

_____

EXERCISE FOR SUPPORTIVE TOPIC SENTENCES

Cross out the topic sentences that do NOT support the report's statement of purpose:

Statement of Purpose   —   *Why the sky is blue.*

Topic sentences:

The sun shines.

The mountains are snowcapped.

The sky has no clouds.

The forest has many trees.

PROGRESSION OF PARAGRAPHS

Paragraphs may be arranged in three logical sequences:

1. Chronological order (with regard to time)
2. Spatial order (with regard to space)
3. Dynamic order (with regard to value), least to greatest value

Chronological — *Time Organization*

If organized by time, the topic sentences follow the events' actual time progression: In June the team suggested an experiment. July 2nd they began the testing. In August they completed it.

Spatial — *Space Organization*

If organized by space, the topic sentences describe the location of the subject in relation to other subjects. Use words such as <u>beside</u>, <u>near</u>, <u>close</u>, <u>approaching</u>, <u>remote</u>, <u>distant</u>, <u>isolated</u> to relate the topic sentences to each other.

Dynamic — *Value Organization*

Write persuasively. If your points build to a climax, from the weakest to the strongest point, you gradually convince your readers with facts. By creating an arrangement that builds toward your goal, you gently persuade your readers to see your point of view.

> **Paragraphs can be rearranged in three ways:**
> - Word processor program
> - "Cut and Paste"
> - "Circles and Arrows"

With a word processor, moving paragraphs is easy. Without a PC, however, there are two time-tested ways to change paragraphs.

The "cut and paste" method is effective. Simply cut each printed page into its various paragraphs, rearrange, and paste the paragraphs onto another piece of paper in the new order.

The "circles and arrows" system is easier because it does not require scissors. Just draw circles around the paragraphs you want moved, then sketch arrows pointing to their new positions. Be sure to number the paragraphs to keep them in their correct order.

Make Sure Report Has a Conclusion

Remember—reports consist of three things:

1. **INTRODUCTION** — Presents Idea

   The introduction presents your idea with your statement of purpose.

2. **BODY OF REPORT** — Supports Idea

   The evidence in the body of your report supports your idea/purpose.

3. **CONCLUSION** — Proves Idea

   The conclusion proves your idea and statement of purpose.

Just like a pyramid, your statement of purpose is found on top. Below that, supporting that, are the facts of the report's body. Beneath that is the strength of your conclusion.

You persuade your audience with your facts and their arrangement in the paragraphs. However, you CONVINCE your audience with your conclusion. Without a conclusion, your readers feel uncertain. With a conclusion, your readers gain confidence in your findings.

Make Sure Each Paragraph Has a Conclusion

Just as each report needs a concluding paragraph, each paragraph needs a concluding sentence.

Let's review paragraph construction:

- Topic sentence
- Supporting sentences
- Concluding sentence
- Transition to next paragraph

Without a concluding statement at the end of the paragraph, your readers will not be certain they understand your point. Your readers need the paragraph summarized to clarify its point.

A paragraph works the same way a report does:

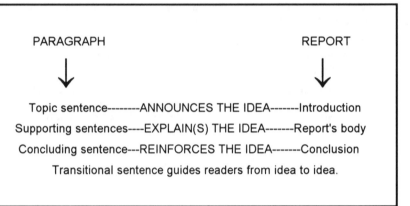

PARAGRAPH   REPORT

Topic sentence--------ANNOUNCES THE IDEA-------Introduction
Supporting sentences----EXPLAIN(S) THE IDEA-------Report's body
Concluding sentence---REINFORCES THE IDEA-------Conclusion
Transitional sentence guides readers from idea to idea.

TOPIC SENTENCE   1) Tell them what you're going to tell them

SUPPORTING SENTENCES   2) Tell them

CONCLUDING SENTENCE   3) Tell them what you told them

EXERCISE FOR CONCLUDING SENTENCE

Following are the statement of purpose and the topic sentences. Write a concluding sentence.

Dogs are wonderful companions. They are helpful in retirement homes, giving unconditional love to lonely residents. They add to the general welfare of families, bringing playfulness and joy. They are the constant partners of blind people, acting not only as guide dogs but also as friends.

_____

_____

_____

_____

_____

Use Specific Details to Support Topic Sentences

Keep subject **SMALL**. Be **DETAILED**. Be precise in your writing. Be specific, not general. Supporting sentences should strengthen each topic sentence with exact details.

Keep subject **SMALLER**. Be **MORE DETAILED**. Remember, don't write about the whole; to best communicate your ideas, write in detail about one specific part or area.

Keep subject **SMALLEST**. Be **MOST DETAILED**. Within that limited area, each paragraph should describe one aspect of your report. Within each paragraph, all the supporting sentences should describe _that_ paragraph's topic sentence.

> **DON'T WRITE ABOUT THE WHOLE PIE;
> ONLY DESCRIBE ONE SMALL SLICE.**

Don't use broad, general statements that are vague. Be specific.

EXERCISE FOR SPECIFIC SUPPORTING DETAILS

Following is a paragraph that contains vague, general details. Rewrite it to make the details more specific:

> Dogs are lovable creatures. They give lots of affection. They love everyone all the time. Everyone loves dogs a lot. Dogs are, indeed, man's best friend.

_____

_____

_____

Leave Out Unrelated Sentences OR Begin New Paragraphs

Leave out supporting sentences that stray from the main idea of your topic sentence. Don't confuse your readers by combining several ideas in one paragraph.

If a supporting sentence is not related to the topic sentence, decide upon its importance. If the supporting sentence is weak, cross it out. If it introduces a new idea, use it as the topic sentence for another paragraph.

- Unimportant   —   Leave out of paragraph
- Important   —   Begin a new paragraph

Use Transitions

Like mayonnaise on a sandwich, transitions help the readers to slide from one idea to the next. Transitions allow sentences to flow more easily. They let the readers follow your thoughts smoothly from paragraph to paragraph.

> For more information in regard to writing paragraphs, refer to the **PARAGRAPHS AND PARANOIA** section. **CHAPTER 11**

Sentences

KEEP SENTENCES SHORT

If each paragraph is a meal, each sentence is a mouthful.

Don't give your readers too much to "chew" in each mouthful. In other words, don't make your sentences so long that your readers can't understand your idea.

On the other hand, don't leave your readers "hungry." Be sure to feed your readers information. Make sure each sentence is a complete thought that adds information by introducing, supporting, or concluding the main idea of the paragraph.

VARY SENTENCE STRUCTURES

Subject, Verb, Object.

Subject, Verb, Object.

SVO is boring!!

Change your sentence structures for variety.
It will keep your readers interested in your ideas.

Which of the following paragraphs would YOU prefer to read?

1. *The boy went home. He opened a book. He read it. His dog sat down. They were content.*

2. *As soon as the boy went home, he opened a book and began reading. After his dog joined him, they were both content.*

The *first* paragraph contains nothing but simple sentences: *The boy* (subject) *went* (verb) *home* (object). SVO. SVO. SVO. SVO.

The *second* paragraph contains sentences that have either been connected or used in combination with transitions. This leads us to the next topic: Combining sentences.

COMBINE SENTENCES

Combine sentences if they repeat similar ideas. This can be done in several ways.

Simple sentences can be connected with coordinating conjunctions (**and, but, or, nor, for, yet**) and a comma.

Other times simple sentences can be linked together by using dependent clauses or phrases. Sentences can be combined into compound, complex, or compound-complex sentences.

For more information, refer to the **CLASSIFICATION** segment of the **SENTENCES AND THEIR CRAFTSMANSHIP** section. **CHAPTER 10**

HAVE CONCLUDING SENTENCE

The concluding sentence MAKES the point, reinforces the idea. Without a concluding sentence, your readers feel uncertain of your meaning. With a concluding sentence, your readers feel they clearly understand your idea.

Remember, the concluding sentence restates or summarizes the idea of the topic sentence. "*Tell them what you told them.*"

Be sure to add a transitional sentence AFTER the concluding sentence, at the end of the paragraph. That way, the readers will know one idea has been completed and now another idea is being announced. Indicate: show your readers what's coming.

Technique

BE OBJECTIVE—NOT SUBJECTIVE

Objective means that all people have the same definition and understanding of a particular set of words. Objective is informative. It provides data for your topic.

Subjective means that each person has a different definition or understanding of a set of words. Subjective is opinionated. It shows your attitude toward your topic.

Both kinds of writing are useful. Objective is preferable when you want to present the facts.
However, if your purpose is to persuade, then be subjective and *slant* your writing to reflect your opinion.

Be consistent. Never mix objective and subjective writing. The combination of the two styles would confuse your readers.

TONE—CONSIDER YOUR WORD CHOICE

These three questions will determine what tone to take:

Remember your audience.	**WHO** *are you writing to?*
Think of your purpose.	**WHY** *are you writing this?*
Consider your subject.	**WHAT** *are you writing about?*

Formal or Informal

Should your tone be formal or informal?

You write a letter to your mother in one tone and an annual report to your stockholders in another. Remember your audience.

You write a resume for a job in one tone and a complaint for the quality control of a purchase in another. Think of your purpose.

You describe the company picnic in one tone and the operation of the computer system in another. Consider your subject.

Notice how word choice changes the tone of the following sentence:

She	**left**	**the room.**
The girl	walked out of	the apartment.
The woman	ran out of	the chamber.
The female	stomped out of	the office.
The old lady	limped from	the study.
The child	escaped from	the school room.

For more information on tone and word choice, see the **REPORTS' TONE: LEVELS OF FORMALITY** section. **CHAPTER 17**

EXERCISE FOR TONE

Rewrite the first sentence to be subjective and informal.
Rewrite the second sentence to be objective and formal.

1. Adore this unsullied atmosphere.

_____

2. Vegetables are good for you.

_____

PLACE WORDS CORRECTLY FOR EMPHASIS

Check for confusing word order. Readers can misunderstand your meaning when words are misplaced. To emphasize your main idea, arrange your words clearly.

Notice how the placement of one word can affect the meaning of the sentence:

Only I think of the company.	—	I'm the only one to remember.
I only think of the company.	—	My loyalty is to the company.
I think only of the company.	—	The company's everything to me.
I think of the only company.	—	There are no other companies.
I think of the company only.	—	I think of no other thing.

PLACE IDEAS CORRECTLY FOR EMPHASIS

Just as word placement shows emphasis, so does idea placement.
Position ideas at one of two places:

1. The   *beginning*   of a sentence
2. The   *end*   of a sentence

> **For the greatest effectiveness, however, place the idea at the END of the sentence. WHY?**
>
> ■   **The sentence builds momentum, builds to a climax**
> ■   **Since it's the last thing they read, the audience will remember it**

USE ACTIVE—NOT PASSIVE—VOICE

> **The passive voice is useful when you WANT the writing to appear vague.**

Passive   —   *Bonuses will be discontinued.*

VAGUE, NONACCUSATORY

Active   —   *Mr. Jones discontinued bonuses.*

CLEAR, ACCUSATORY

(The tone is critical. HE did it!)

EXERCISE FOR ACTIVE VOICE

Rewrite the following sentence using the active voice:

The office was kept neat by the people who cleaned it.

_____

BE CONCISE

Choose your words carefully. Keep words to a minimum, but try to use words that are fresh and original. Avoid cliches.

Cliches are stale phrases that have been used over and over, e.g.,

> *Dog tired. Bone dry. Fit as a fiddle. Looking out for number one.*
> *All in a day's work. Good as new. Good as gold.*

Pick your words more carefully than you pick your friends!

- Use vivid, not vague VOCABULARY
- Use strong VERBS that drive sentences forward
- Use concrete NOUNS to reduce amount of words
- Use as few ADJECTIVES as possible

Don't use word-splurgers like IT, THAT, THERE, WHICH, and WHO. These vague words demand too many more words to explain them.

> **Imagine that words are expensive.**
> **Keep "costs" to a minimum!**

Nuts and Bolts

CHECK FOR ERRORS OR OMISSIONS

- Yours
- Others'

CHECK FOR THESE:

- Spelling
- Punctuation
- Grammar

For more information, refer to the **SENTENCES AND THEIR CRAFTSMANSHIP** section. **CHAPTER 10**

CHECK FOR TYPOS

Last but not least, check for typing errors. Nothing ruins a report like a sloppy display of poor typing skills.

Remember, edit, rewrite, and polish until your writing DISAPPEARS! Leave only your ideas for your readers.

GRAPHICS

OR A PICTURE'S WORTH A THOUSAND WORDS

20

Reports don't need to include graphs, charts, or diagrams; however, graphics do have their advantages in three areas:

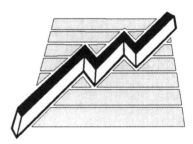

- Dramatic illustration
  Graphics are **exciting!**

- Space restriction
  Graphics are **small!**

- Time limitation
  Graphics are **fast!**

DRAMATIC ILLUSTRATION

Graphics can explain your thoughts more dramatically than words can. Consider graphics a tool to help clarify your ideas or more vividly illustrate changing data.

SPACE RESTRICTION

Space restriction is a factor in deciding whether to use graphics. A huge amount of information can be condensed into one small graph. When space is in short supply, don't tell your audience, SHOW them.

TIME LIMITATION

Visuals are also an effective means of communication when your readers' time is limited. Your audience can grasp your message at a glance. They can SEE what you mean.

> NOTE: **The following graphs do not represent actual data. They are used solely as models.**

TYPES OF GRAPHICS

Two-Scale and One-Scale Graphics are examined in this chapter.

Two-Scale Graphics

- Area
- Grouped Bar
- Line

One-Scale Graphics

- Bar Charts
- Pie
- Exploded Pie

Two-Scale Graphics

Two-scale graphics contain information horizontally → and vertically ↑. Since the information is presented at right angles, it forms a grid between the horizontal and vertical axes in which it is easy to isolate any specific fact.

Area Charts

Area charts are similar to line charts. (See GRAPHIC 1.) The difference is that the lines become the borders of areas that are then shaded to increase the charts' visibility.

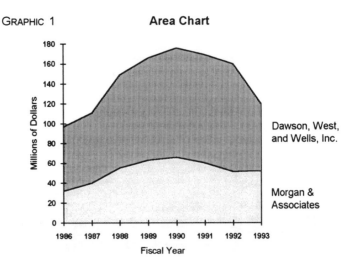

GRAPHIC 1   **Area Chart**

GROUPED BAR CHARTS

Bar charts are exactly that: charts with bars or oblongs that represent facts. Grouped bar charts are bars arranged side-by-side that contrast two data bases that are different yet related. These charts can be horizontal or across the page (see GRAPHIC 2) and vertical or up-and-down the page (see GRAPHIC 3). Both are effective; the choice is yours.

GRAPHIC 2   **Horizontal Grouped Bar Chart**

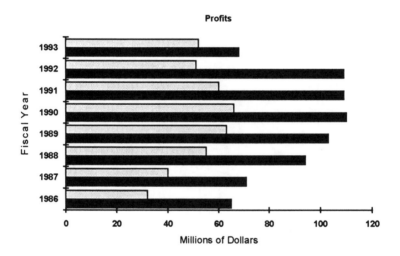

GRAPHIC 3   **Vertical Grouped Bar Chart**

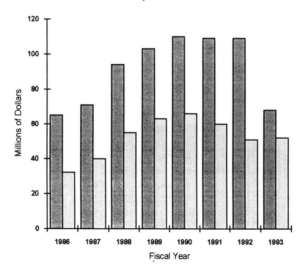

Line Charts

Line charts, sometimes called curve charts, connect a series of dots with a line. (See GRAPHIC 4.) Each dot represents a fact. Depending upon the chart's information, the line can be jagged and irregular or smooth and flat.

Because each dot shows the data at that moment, line charts are most effective in showing time-related change. The chart could show daily, monthly, or yearly increments of change.

GRAPHIC 4 **Line Chart**

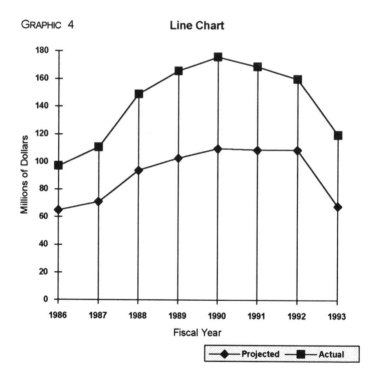

One-Scale Graphics

One-scale graphics do not form a grid of criss-crossing facts. They are one dimensional, useful but limited in their ability to show large amounts of information. Pie charts and exploding pie charts are the most common one-scale graphics. However, simple bar charts *may* be grouped into this class.

BAR CHARTS

Bar Charts may be grouped into the one-scale graphics class if two things occur:

1. The bars offer information on one scale or axis only, e.g., horizontal (see GRAPHIC 5) **OR** vertical (see GRAPHIC 6) **(NOT BOTH)**.
2. The bars' other scale value is used to list items only.

GRAPHIC 5 **Horizontal Bar Chart**

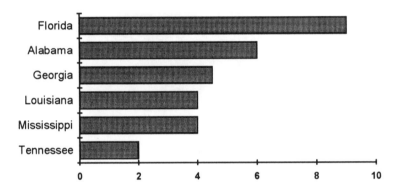

GRAPHIC 6 **Vertical Bar Chart**

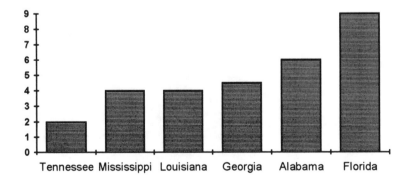

American Business English

PIE CHARTS

Pie charts are round and divided into slices. (See GRAPHIC 7.) These charts are effective for portraying percentiles or parts of a whole, but they do not lend themselves to representing change as well as grouped bar or line charts do. Pie charts cannot compare data; they can only show ratio and proportion.

GRAPHIC 7   **Pie Chart**

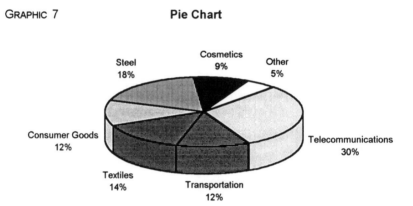

EXPLODED PIE CHARTS

Exploded pie charts are also round with one or more wedges "blasted" outward from the center; the exploded areas are the focus of the graph. (See GRAPHIC 8.) The data of these emphasized parts is then compared to the data from the rest of the pie.

GRAPHIC 8   **Exploded Pie Chart**

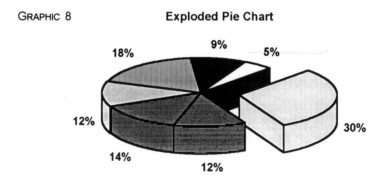

GRAPH WRITING TECHNIQUES

Charts are very effective methods of presenting material. However, three techniques are especially important for graphs:

1. Scale
2. Explanation
3. Titles

Graph Scale

Graph scale is a ratio showing the proportion of one thing to another. Scale is the most important factor of a graph. Scale determines audience reaction, so plan it based upon audience approval. Give your readers what they want to see. Or better yet, give your readers what YOU WANT them to see. Notice the different viewpoints in the following graphs.

If a country's trade balance has a surplus of US $7.5 billion over a year's time, a graph using a scale of figures for ONE year depicts a **FLAT** graph which **APPEARS** to show little growth. (See GRAPHIC 9.)

What reaction do you think the audience will have?

GRAPHIC 9   **1986 Trade Surplus Graph**

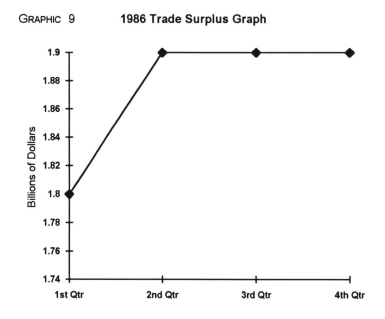

However, the same US $7.5 billion, if shown over a SIX-year period (1984–89) portrays a **RISING** graph that **APPEARS** to indicate a much higher trade surplus. (See GRAPHIC 10.)

What reaction do you think the audience will have now?

GRAPHIC 10   **Trade Surplus**

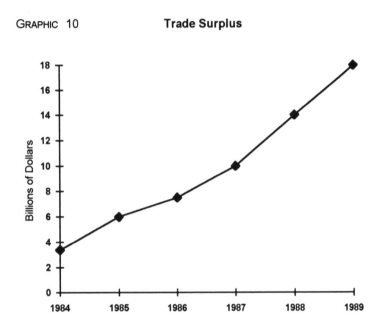

Graph scale can make things seem better or worse than they are. Because appearances are so important, use scale to your advantage. Choose your scale carefully. Think of your readers' reactions before planning your graphs.

Graph Explanation

Even with graphics, words are the chief consideration. Without words, graphs are meaningless. Write your graph measurements or explanations clearly, so your audience can understand.

Useful Graph Jargon

VERBS	NOUNS
to climb	a climb
to ascend	an ascent
to rise	a rise
to fall	a fall
to decline	a decline
to plunge	a plunge
to improve	an improvement
to recover	a recovery
to increase	an increase
to decrease	a decrease
to worsen	a slip
to deteriorate	a dip
to project	a projection
to forecast	a forecast
to predict	a prediction

ADJECTIVES	ADVERBS	DESCRIPTION
slight	slightly	insignificant
sharp	sharply	fast, big
abrupt	abruptly	sudden
rapid	rapidly	very fast
sudden	suddenly	without warning
dramatic	dramatically	fast, very big
climactic	climactically	fastest, largest
tense	tensely	anxious change
calm	calmly	no sudden change
flat	flatly	without change
steady	steadily	no change
constant	constantly	no change
even	evenly	no sudden change
substantial	substantially	large change

Keep graphs to the point. Too much information will confuse your audience. It's better to use two simple graphs than to use one large, complex graph. Remember, the main goal is to communicate information, not impress your audience with your skills.

Keep graphs simple. Don't add so many technical details to your graph that it perplexes your audience. Add enough information for your audience to understand, but not so much that it confuses them.

Caption Expressions for Reasons/Results

Give brief reasons for results:

The increase in available housing------------------lower land values.

> resulted in
>
> caused
>
> led to
>
> precipitated
>
> produced
>
> generated

Conclude brief results from reasons:

Lower land values-------------------------increased available housing.

> resulted from
>
> occurred from
>
> were caused by
>
> were due to
>
> were generated by
>
> were produced by

Merge your graphs into your written report. Don't expect your audience to turn to page 27 to look at a graph, while reading page three. The idea of graphs is to make it **EASIER**, not harder, for your readers to absorb your information.

Graph Titles

Entitling graphs requires thought. Instead of simply numbering or naming your graphs, describe the subject and/or conclusions of the graphs in your titles. This increases their informative value.

Sometimes, related graphs are connected by a series of captions.

Captions are short explanations. A series of captions is called Statement or Narrative Labeling. It's an effective space-saver. However, use in moderation. Too many graphs will overpower the report, and the audience will ignore the written portion.

GRAPHIC 11

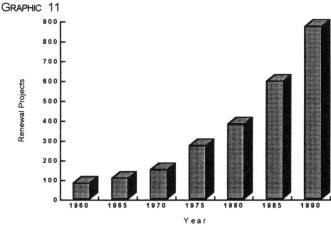

URBAN RENEWAL projects...

GRAPHIC 12

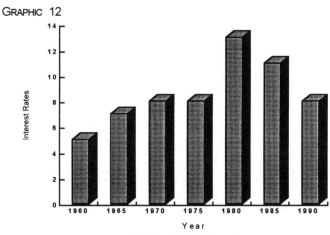

...and INTEREST RATES...

GRAPHIC 13

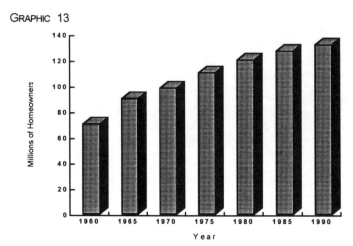

...have helped more people to become HOMEOWNERS...

GRAPHIC 14

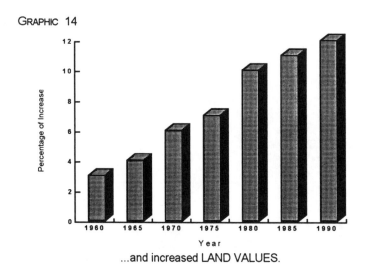

...and increased LAND VALUES.

Less is more. The fewer the graphs, the greater the impact of each. Just be sure that your graphs relate closely to your subject and that they are titled or captioned effectively.

EXERCISE FOR GRAPHS

Draw and caption the following line graph (GRAPHIC 15).
Decide who your audience will be before you plan your graph!
Use one of these examples:

1. Show your yearly earnings

2. Project next year's gross income

3. Predict next year's net income

4. Show your department's productivity

GRAPHIC 15   **Graph Exercise**

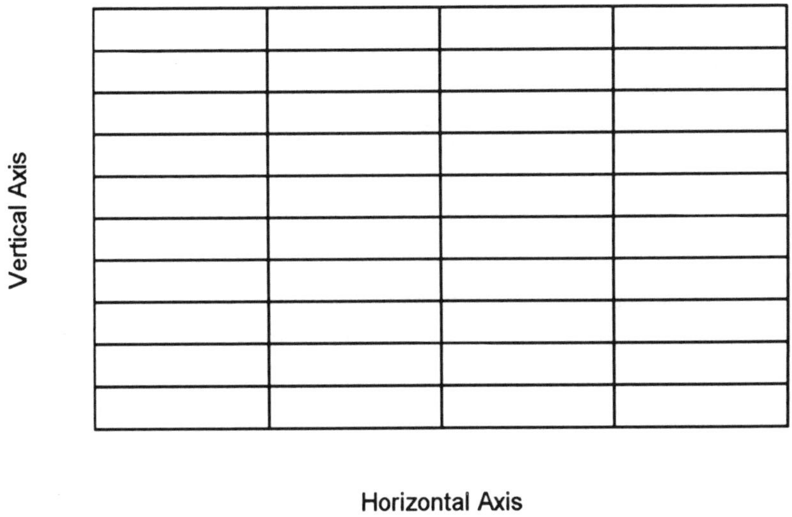

Vertical Axis

Horizontal Axis

ANSWER KEY

Chapter 1

EXERCISE FOR CONCRETE AND ABSTRACT WORDS (p. 3)

Any words beginning with the letter **S** are concrete THINGS.

The other words are all abstract IDEAS, open to interpretation.

EXERCISE FOR GENERAL TO SPECIFIC ORDER (p. 3)

2	tall people
4	a tall boy
3	tall boys
9	John Smith, who is 6' 3" tall
1	tallness
5	the tall boy
7	the boy who is 6' 3" tall
8	John, who is 6' 3" tall
6	a boy 6' 3" tall

Chapter 4

EXERCISE FOR ACTIVE/PASSIVE VOICES (p. 18)

1. Sam wrote the report because Jules had made the speech.

2. The driver waxed and polished the car.

3. All her colleagues knew Joan, and everyone respected her.

4. He wore the new tuxedo to the business function.

5. The FBI dropped the case against the embezzler because of lack of evidence.

Chapter 7

EXERCISE FOR COMMAS (p. 29)

1. The midwestern states involved in our project are Wisconsin, Michigan, Illinois, and Indiana.

2. The truck approached a wide, smooth span of highway.

3. The company invested wisely, and the dividends paid well.

4. Ms. Jones ordered coffee and eggs and toast for breakfast.

5. The insurance policy covered disability, maternity leave, and durable equipment in the employees' benefits.

EXERCISE FOR SEMICOLONS (p. 32)

1. In the morning, I like melon; I prefer apples.

   Comma splice

2. He got up early; he dressed before breakfast.

   Exchange the comma <u>and the AND</u> for the semicolon

3. They had lunch; then they went back to work.

   Run on sentence

4. The bus was crowded; the taxis wouldn't stop.

   <u>And</u> is unnecessary

5. Sam ordered a hamburger, fries, and a coke; Jane ordered a salad, a croissant and tea; Tim only wanted coffee.

   Semicolons are needed in a series with commas

EXERCISE FOR COLONS AND DASHES (p. 34)

1. Our bowling team—there are eight of us—went to the bowling alley at 7:30 and stayed until 10:00.

2. John bought the book *How to Cook: A Manual for Bachelors*—just the kind of book he needs.

3. The XYZ Company ordered the following: chairs, desks, computers.

4. Tom needed everything—a refrigerator, a stove, a washing machine.

5. Dear Mrs. Jones: Dear Susan,

EXERCISE FOR QUESTION, EXCLAMATION, AND QUOTATION MARKS (p. 38)

1. She asked, "Are you ready?"
2. Were you ready when she asked, "Are you ready"**?**
3. Get going if you don't want to be late!
4. "Hurry up!" he said.
5. I was nervous when he shouted, "No!"

EXERCISE FOR APOSTROPHES (p. 41)

1. It's Peter's car.
2. They're part of John's group.
3. It's time to celebrate '97.
4. Isn't that Jane's house?
5. Didn't they say it was hers?

Chapter 8

EXERCISE FOR WORDINESS (p. 48)

Call, don't write.

EXERCISE FOR THE FINAL E (p. 52)

1. leaving   2. sneezing 3. preferably 4. sharing 5. curable

EXERCISE FOR DOUBLING FINAL CONSONANTS (p. 52)

1. curing   2. debriefing   3. getting   4. meeting   5. trapping

EXERCISE FOR IE AND EI (p. 55)

1. achieve   2. friend   3. foreign   4. niece   5. weird

Chapter 9

EXERCISE FOR TIME: PREPOSITION (p. 72)

AT	ON	IN
7 o'clock	Tuesday	April
noon	Sunday	1994
Christmas	Monday evening	summer
6:20	the first	five minutes
quarter past two	Friday	1856
half past one		2004
midnight		autumn
		the morning

Chapter 11

EXERCISE FOR PARAGRAPH PROGRESSION (p. 92)

These topic sentences are arranged in a dynamic progression, beginning from the weakest point and ending with the strongest:

Statement of Purpose—Why you should purchase THIS stock.

Topic Sentences

1	—it usually shows a yearly profit.
2	—it gives dividends.
3	—it is underrated.
4	—it will split soon.

EXERCISE II FOR TOPIC SENTENCES (p. 93)

Following is a topic sentence for the supporting sentences:

Owning property is the best hedge against inflation.
Owning your home saves money, because it invests the mortgage payments, instead of wasting the rental payments. Whether the stock market goes up or down, land values increase at a relatively constant rate. Currencies can spiral in value or devaluate. However, owning property is the best barrier to inflation.

EXERCISE II FOR SUPPORTING SENTENCES (p. 94)

The supporting sentences that do *NOT* belong in the following paragraph are italicized:

A house is a home. Where you live is more than <u>just</u> a residence. It is a refuge to which you can escape from the problems of the world. Home is a place where loved ones offer support. *Houses are good investments.* A house is a retreat from the difficulties of the workplace, school, the office. *Many people do not have homes of their own.* Indeed, your house is much more than a place to hang your hat; it's home.

EXERCISE FOR CONCLUDING SENTENCE (p. 95)

Following is a completed paragraph consisting of a topic sentence, supporting sentences, and *a concluding sentence*:

Learning to write a paragraph is easy. You need only to introduce your subject with a topic sentence. Then you write several detailed sentences to support your idea. Finally you write a concluding sentence that restates your topic sentence. *As you can see for yourself, learning to write a paragraph is easy.*

EXERCISE FOR IDEA EMPHASIS (p. 102)

This sentence places the most important idea at its end:

The reason we should bid is to get the contract.

Chapter 18

EXERCISE FOR PROCESS—TEA BREWING (p. 184)

COLUMN A	COLUMN B
FIRST	Fill the tea kettle with water
SECOND	Boil the water
NEXT	Warm the teapot for a while
AFTER THAT	Put some tea into the teapot
THEN	Fill teapot with boiling water
NEXT	Leave the teapot
AFTER THIS	Pour the tea into the teacup
FINALLY	Pour the milk into the teacup

Chapter 19

EXERCISE FOR DESCRIPTIVE TOPIC SENTENCE (p. 195)

Following is a paragraph which contains a descriptive topic sentence, supporting sentences, and a concluding sentence.

Further sale of automobiles in this city should be stopped. Air pollution is at record levels. Traffic jams are common. Rush hour is a disaster. The cars are backed-up for miles. Road intersections are gridlocked; cars can't cross the street in either direction. Parking is even worse. Parking space was not a consideration in the construction of the city. This boom town was unprepared for such fast growth. With too many cars already, no other automobiles should be allowed in the city.

EXERCISE FOR SUPPORTIVE TOPIC SENTENCES (p. 196)

These topic sentences support the report's statement of purpose:

Statement of Purpose	—Why the sky is blue.
Topic sentences:	—The sun shines.
	—The sky has no clouds.

EXERCISE FOR CONCLUDING SENTENCE **(p. 198)**

Following are the statement of purpose, the topic sentences, and a concluding sentence.

Dogs are wonderful companions. They are helpful in retirement homes, giving unconditional love to lonely residents. They add to the general welfare of families, bringing playfulness and joy. They are the constant partners of blind people, acting not only as guide dogs but also as friends. *Dogs, indeed, are man's best friend.*

EXERCISE FOR SPECIFIC SUPPORTING DETAILS **(p. 199)**

Following is a rewritten paragraph that contains more specific details:

Dogs are lovable creatures. Because of their affection, they are helpful in retirement homes, giving unconditional love to lonely residents. Their love adds to the general welfare of families, bringing playfulness and joy. If not man's *best* friend, dogs are, indeed, lovable creatures.

EXERCISE FOR TONE **(p. 203)**

1. I like fresh air.
SUBJECTIVE & INFORMAL

2. Organically grown legumes are nutritious.
OBJECTIVE & FORMAL

EXERCISE FOR ACTIVE VOICE **(p. 204)**

The following sentence uses the active voice:

The cleaners kept the office neat.

GLOSSARY

Abbreviation	—	is a shortened spelling of a word (*adj.* instead of *adjective*).
Abstract	—	as adjective is a thought, not a thing.
		as noun is a summary of a report or manual.
Acronym	—	is a word spelled from the initials of other words (*NATO for North Atlantic Treaty Organization*).
Active voice	—	describes an action done BY its subject.
Agenda	—	is a list of topics to discuss at a meeting.
Agreement	—	is the unity of nouns and verbs in number and person (*he is* or *they are*).
Asterisk	—	is a mark (*) used to draw attention to a feature.
Audience	—	is a group of readers or listeners.
Bibliography	—	is a list of books or articles used as references.
Brainstorming	—	is a discussion among people to create ideas.
Bullet	—	is a mark (■) used to draw attention to a feature.
Call to action	—	is a suggestion that causes people to act.
Caption	—	is a title explaining a picture.
Clustering	—	is a picture of ideas, with new ideas surrounding the original ideas.
Comparison	—	compares subjects that are similar.
Concluding sentence	—	is the final sentence of a paragraph.
Concrete	—	is a thing, not a thought.
Contrast	—	contrasts subjects that are different.
Coordinators	—	also coordinating conjunctions, are the words *and, but, or, nor, for, yet*. Used with a comma, they can join two sentences.
Correspondence	—	is written communication, usually letters.
Deductive reasoning	—	begins with general ideas and develops to specific details.

Editing	—	is the locating and correcting of errors in writing.
Fallacies	—	are errors in reasoning.
Free-writing	—	is writing without a specific topic in mind.
General	—	is vague, not detailed or specific.
Header	—	is another word for title.
Indirect	—	is vague, not direct or straightforward.
Inductive reasoning	—	begins with specific details and develops to general ideas.
Infer	—	is to conclude or presume by reasoning.
Jargon	—	is language that is either VERY specific to a particular group or is pretentious.
Key words	—	are words or phrases that help readers understand precise information.
Limning	—	is similar to outlining. It uses a few words to organize thoughts.
Minutes	—	are the formal records of meetings.
Objective	—	is factual without personal opinion.
Outline	—	uses a few words to organize thoughts.
Paragraph	—	is a group of sentences that describes one idea.
Parallel	—	shows similarity between grammatical patterns (*eats, drinks, talks*, NOT eats, talking, drank).
Paraphrase	—	is to express another way, instead of quoting.
Passive voice	—	describes an action done TO its subject.
Persuade	—	is to convince through words or action.
Point of view	—	is a person's attitude or opinion.
Prefix	—	is a letter or letters that come before a word (*dis*prove).
Punctuation	—	is the use of marks to indicate direction in writing (,.;:?!").
Query	—	is a question or a letter that asks a question.
Read between the lines	—	is to interpret the deeper meaning of the writing.

Rewriting	—	is correcting and writing a material again.
Rough draft	—	is the first attempt at writing a report or letter.
Solicited	—	means requested.
Specific	—	is precise, exact.
Spread-sheet writing	—	is a picture of ideas, with new ideas spreading outward from the original idea.
Statement of purpose	—	is the announcement of your meaning.
Subjective	—	is not factual. It reflects personal opinion.
Subordinators	—	also known as subordinating conjunctions, they are words that begin subordinate clauses or phrases.
Suffix	—	is a letter or letters that come after a word (worth*less*).
Supporting sentence	—	is a sentence in a paragraph that strengthens the main idea of the topic sentence.
Syllogism	—	uses two premises and a conclusion to reason a resolution.
Synopsis	—	is a summary.
Tactics	—	are plans and strategies.
Tone	—	is the general attitude or style of writing.
Topic	—	is a subject or main idea.
Topic sentence	—	is also called the main idea sentence.
Transition	—	is a word or sentence that leads readers from one idea to the next.
Typography	—	is the selection of type or characters for printed material.

RECOMMENDED READING

The following list of books contains a wealth of information.
I strongly recommend reading each publication.

Adelstein, Michael E. *Contemporary Business Writing*. New York:
Random, 1971.

Andrews, Clarence A. *Technical and Business Writing*. Boston:
Houghton, 1975.

Aurner, Robert R. *Effective Communication in Business*. 4th ed.
Cincinnati: South Western, 1958.

Azar, Betty Schrampfer. *Understanding and Using English Grammar*. 2d
ed. Englewood Cliffs: Prentice, 1989.

Berkoff, N. A. *English Grammar and Structure*. 1963. Taipei, ROC:
Ch'eng Wen, 1976.

Blass, Laurie, and Joy Durighello. *From Concept to Composition*. 1985.
Taipei, ROC: Crane, 1985.

Blumenthal, Joseph C. *English 3200: A Programmed Course in Grammar
and Usage*. New York: Harcourt, 1960.

Brandt, Sue R. *How to Write a Report*. 1968. New York: Watts, 1986.

Campbell, Robert Ronald. *English Composition for Foreign Students*.
London: Longmans, Green, 1938.

Casanave, Christine Pearson. *Strategies For Readers*. Englewood Cliffs:
Prentice, 1986.

Cool, Lis Collier. *How to Write Irresistible Query Letters*. Cincinnati: F&W
Publications, 1987.

Eddings, Claire Neff. *Secretary's Complete Model Letter Handbook*. 21st
ed. Engelwood Cliffs: Prentice, 1977.

Fear, David E., and Gerald J. Schiffhorst. *Short English Handbook/2*. 2d
ed. Glenview, Ill.: Scott, 1982.

Geffner, Andrea B. *How to Write Better Business Letters*. Woodbury,
    N.Y.: Barron's Educational Series, 1982.

Gibaldi, Joseph, and Walter S. Achtert. *MLA Handbook for Writers of
    Research Papers*. New York: MLA, 1988.

Howard, V. A., and J. H. Barton. *Thinking on Paper*. New York: Morrow,
    1986.

Leggett, Glenn, C. David Mead, and William Charvat. *Prentice-Hall
    Handbook for Writers*. 7th ed. Englewood Cliffs: Prentice,
    1978.

Means, Beth, and Lindy Lindner. *Everything You Needed to Learn about
    Writing in High School—But a) you were in love b) you have
    forgotten c) you fell asleep d) they didn't tell you e) all of the
    above*. Englewood, Colo.: Libraries Unlimited, 1989.

Random House Dictionary of the English Language. 2d ed. New York:
    Random, 1987.

Reed, Jeanne. *Business English*. 1966. Taipei, ROC: University Book,
    1968.

Robertson, H. O., and Vernal H. Carmichael. *Business Letter English*.
    New York: McGraw, 1957.

Ross-Larson, Bruce. *Edit Yourself*. New York: Norton, 1982.

Shurter, Robert L. *Written Communication in Business*. 1971. Taiwan,
    ROC: McGraw, 1979.

Slatkin, Elizabeth. *How to Write a Manual*. Berkeley: Ten Speed, 1991.

Tressler, J. C., and Maurice C. Lipman. *Business English in Action*.
    2d ed. Boston: Heath, 1957.

Warren, Thomas L. *Purpose, Process, and Form*. Belmont, Calif.:
    Wadsworth, 1985.

Willis, Hulon. *A Brief Handbook of English*. 1975. Taipei, ROC: Ch'eng
    Wen, 1976.

Zinsser, William. *Writing to Learn*. New York: Harper, 1988.